Milton's Knowledge of Music

BY SIGMUND SPAETH

Foreword by Warner G. Rice

ANN ARBOR PAPERBACKS
THE UNIVERSITY OF MICHIGAN PRESS

First edition as an Ann Arbor Paperback 1963
Foreword copyright © by The University of Michigan 1963
All rights reserved
First published by Princeton University Library 1913
Published in the United States of America by
The University of Michigan Press and simultaneously
in Toronto, Canada, by Ambassador Books Limited
Manufactured in the United States of America

FOREWORD

Dr. Sigmund Spaeth has devoted most of a long life to the transmission to thousands of potential music lovers of his own enthusiasm for the musical arts. He has been a composer and arranger of scores, a performer, a broadcaster, a leading figure in a dozen professional societies, a music editor for newspapers and magazines, and the Tune Detective of radio, television, and cinema. Through the authorship of more than thirty books he has reached a large popular audience. But his first published monograph, which took form as a Princeton dissertation, was intended for scholars, and bears witness not only to his wide learning, but also to his thoroughness in research and to full understanding of his subject.

Since the appearance in 1913 of *Milton's Knowledge of Music* enormous efforts have been expended in the study of the poet and of many matters relating to him. In a half century there have been changes of taste and outlook; and at present many critics, scrutinizing each line of Milton's text with the aid of the accumulated apparatus of centuries, and bringing to bear many new theories drawn from the behavioral sciences, find themselves repeating, in a more sophisticated form, the strictures which were current a century ago. That is, they regard as inacceptable Milton's God and Milton's religion and reject as inadequate his understanding of the human condition. It is probably inevitable that this should be so in an age which is leaving the past behind at an accelerated rate. Certainly, however, the chief participants in the great Milton revival which took place a generation ago were more just to their subject. Scholars like James Holly Hanford, Merritt Y. Hughes, Douglas Bush, C. S. Lewis, and A. S. P. Woodhouse firmly established Milton in the great tradition of Christian humanism, and interpreted his works in that context. It is greatly to Dr. Spaeth's credit that he made an early contribution to this endeavor by demonstrating how enlightened and liberal Milton's Puritanism really was, and by tracing from its sources Milton's concept of the place which music should occupy in the life of man.

During recent years scholars have added greatly to the literature of music history and musicology. It is clear, nevertheless, that the lines which Dr. Spaeth laid down so firmly and so knowledgeably were drawn right. The student of Milton will find only a few items which notably augment the material and ideas presented in the pioneer study. He will wish to consult Professor Hughes's essay on "Lydian Airs" in the fortieth volume of *Modern Language Notes,* and to look up such items as numbers 1081, 1270, 1364, 1513, and 1543 in Calvin Huckabay's *John Milton: A Bibliographical Supplement, 1929–1957.* Here, and in Gretchen L. Finney's *Musical Backgrounds for English Literature: 1580–1650* (Rutgers University Press, 1961), he will find additional material on Milton and music; but he will remain grateful for the basic data and interpretations which Dr. Spaeth provided—and for this reprint, which again makes them readily available.

Warner G. Rice

CONTENTS

ENGLISH MUSIC
IN THE SEVENTEENTH CENTURY

A great man cannot be studied apart from his natural surroundings. John Milton, as a poet, as a musician, or as a highly developed example of the alliance of both arts, fails to reveal his true significance except as he is regarded in the light of his environment and of the characteristics of his own time. Before attempting an exposition of Milton's knowledge of music, therefore, it becomes necessary to examine and interpret the general conditions of music which prevailed in his time, to analyze the popular taste, and to become acquainted with the representative composers and their style of work.

As far back as the reign of Henry VIII a golden age of English music had begun. At that time there was little real musical activity on the continent, and that little was sporadic and inconstant, without order or design. The Flemings, it is true, had displayed marked ability, particularly in the development of the madrigal form, but their efforts were so widely scattered, and their composers forced to cater to such a variety of tastes, that a really characteristic style was never developed. Germany produced only one or two good composers. Italy, preoccupied with her rediscovery of the ancient world, contributed nothing of her own to the world's music, but satisfied herself, as did most of the other continental nations, with the work of imported Flemish composers. In England alone was there a distinct native school. This was, of course, largely due to the encouragement and example of Henry VIII himself, who was a composer and performer of ability. But aside from the efforts of individuals, there was a national spirit and a consistency of style in English music entirely lacking in that of other countries. The English people, as a whole, seem to have acquired a definite taste earlier than the other nations, and the means of gratifying this taste were not wanting. Composers and performers alike were plentiful, and, while no great individual reputations were made, a national school was established which preserved its characteristics and retained its distinctiveness for more than a century. The climax of this long sustained activity in music came, as may be supposed, in the time of Elizabeth, when English music and English literature alike reached their highest level.[1]

In vocal music, it is true, Italy had, by the end of the sixteenth century, taken the lead, through the work of Palestrina and his successors. But the English instrumental music was still supreme.[2]

Characteristic of the Elizabethan period was the madrigal form, which, while adapted from the Flemish and Italian schools, attained the widest popularity in England. Madrigals were originally vocal works, written in counterpoint, without accompaniment.[3] The number of parts varied, but was commonly four or five. The words were of little importance, and frequently consisted of meaningless phrases repeated over and over. Such a

[1] I make this statement with no thought of detracting in the least from the reputation of Purcell, who was beyond a doubt England's greatest musician. He was, however, an individual genius rather than the product of a school. The English music of his time was, on the whole, inferior to that which had gone before.

[2] For the history of English music in the sixteenth century, see Hawkins, *History of Music*, vol. 3 ; Burney, *History of Music*, vol. 3 ; Henry Davey, *History of English Music*, chaps. 3, 4, 5.

[3] See definition in Grove's *Dictionary*.

style of song, it may be imagined, differed little from instrumental music. In fact, the later polyphonic instrumental music was the direct outgrowth of the madrigal school. The same characteristics of counterpoint and of complex harmonies are to be found in the sacred music of the day. The compositions of Tallis and Tye served as models for succeeding generations. For it was the sacred music of the Elizabethans that proved most worthy of enduring fame. It must not be assumed, however, that any very distinct lines were drawn between the sacred and the secular, or even between the popular and the " skilled " music. All rested upon a common foundation, the famous ecclesiastical modes of Saint Gregory, which, in turn, corresponded to the Greek scales of the diatonic genus.

It will be seen that Elizabethan music was of the formal rather than of the emotional type. The mathematical formulas which had been handed down from ancient times still governed the structure of music. The test applied to a composition was not " Is it beautiful ? " but rather " Is it correct ? " and the critical conclusion usually took the form, " If it is correct, it must be beautiful," rather than " If it is beautiful, it must be correct." In spite of its apparent spontaneity Elizabethan music depended less upon natural instincts, than upon artificial laws and regulations. It would be wrong to assume, however, that this condition of affairs resulted in a musical aristocracy, composed only of the highly educated. As a matter of fact, the ordinary laws of composition were so simple as to be within the grasp of any one. Thus a formal style of music prevailed among all classes, the elements of which were the same for the popular ballad-writer, as for the severely correct composer of sacred music.[1]

[1] Wooldridge, in his Preface to Chappell's *Old English Popular Music* (p. xii), particularly emphasizes the free use of the eccles-

With a knowledge of music thus within the reach of all men, it is not surprising that, in the recognized composers of the day, versatility was of all things desirable. A typical genius of the time was William Byrd, a man who achieved astonishing success both as composer and performer on various instruments, and who could turn his hand to every style of sacred and secular music.[1]

Thomas Morley, author of *A Plain and Easy Introduction to Practical Music*, showed almost equal versatility. Not only did his great work remain the standard text-book of musical theory for generations, but his madrigals and other compositions attained a wide popularity.[2]

There were many other composers similar to these, and all were versatile, highly inventive, and prolific.

The seventeenth century, therefore, received a musical heritage of the highest value, and it was not slow in putting this capital to use. For music had now become not only the most popular art in England, but a recognized and universally respected science. Never had the interest in music been so general and spontaneous. It was not

iastical modes in the composition of all kinds of secular music until about the second decade of the seventeenth century. " The popular treatment of them differed in no essential respect from the ecclesiastical ; and the nameless authors of the ballad tunes, for anything their work shows to the contrary, might well have been the very men whom we know and honor as composers for the church. Even in such a matter as the choice of scales to write in, there is no difference ; the modes most used and those most neglected being in both kinds of music the same."

[1] Henry Peacham in his *Compleat Gentleman*, p. 100, eulogizes particularly the sacred music of " our Phoenix Mr. William Byrd, whom, in that kind, I know not whether any may equall, I am sure none excell, even by the judgement of France and Italy, who are very sparing in the commendation of strangers, in regard of that conceipt they hold of themselves."

[2] Grove's *Dict.* s. v. *Morley.*

a period of great composers, for under the existing conditions these were not necessary. It was rather a time of universal participation in music, when all men, no matter what their condition or ability, could in some way be active in the art. This fact must be understood by one who would appreciate the spirit of the seventeenth century music. Through the activity of the Elizabethans a musical atmosphere had been created in which men of all classes moved. No gentleman could claim to be well-educated unless he possessed considerable musical skill. Peacham evidently considered his requirements very modest when he said: " I desire no more in you than to sing your part sure and at the first sight; withall, to play the same upon your Viol, or the exercise of the Lute, privately to yourself." [1]

Indeed, the ability to perform on some instrument, or at least to sing a part at sight, was taken as a matter of course. It is so regarded in the opening dialogue of Morley's treatise, in which one of the interlocutors, having been " earnestly requested to sing," says: " But when, after many excuses, I protested unfainedly that I could not, everyone began to wonder; yea some whispered to others, demanding how I was brought up." [2] It was evidently the custom at social gatherings for the whole company to join in song. The music-books of the day were printed with the parts facing in different directions, so that the singers could gather round a table and sing all the parts from one book.[3] Various instruments, particularly the conventional " chest of viols," formed a necessary part of the furnishing of a gentleman's household. It was nothing unusual for amateurs to produce

---

[1] *Compleat Gentleman*, p. 100.
[2] Morley, p. 1.
[3] See the illustrations in Morley, pp. 254-257.

compositions of real merit, and the art of improvisation, both instrumental and vocal, was highly developed.

The popularity of music was by no means confined to the aristocracy. As in the sixteenth century, little distinction was made between "skilled" and "popular" music. The common people had not only their folk-songs and ballads, but glees, rounds, catches, and the various styles of country dance as well. There was a great demand for servants or apprentices of musical ability.[1] " Tinkers sang catches ; milkmaids sang ballads ; carters whistled ; each trade, and even the beggars, had their special songs ; the base-viol hung in the drawing-room for the amusement of waiting visitors ; and the lute, cittern, and virginals, for the amusement of waiting customers, were the necessary furniture of the barber's shop. They had music at dinner ; music at supper ; music at weddings ; music at funerals ; music at night ; music at dawn ; music at work ; music at play. He who felt not, in some degree, its soothing influences, was viewed as a morose unsocial being, whose converse ought to be shunned and regarded with suspicion and distrust."[2]

Curiously enough, among the common people as well as in the cultured classes, music seemed to appeal rather to the ingenuity than to the emotions of men. It was the science and the theory of the structure of music rather than its mere effect on the feelings that attracted interest. To the uneducated mind, the mysteries of a " round," with its mathematical accuracy, possessed a fascination which the most melodious of folk-songs could not equal. To a more highly developed intellect the laws of harmony, " proportion," and counterpoint provided endless material for thought. Peacham

[1] See the interesting note on this subject, Chappell 1. 1.

[2] Chappell 1. 59. Cf. also the references which he gives on pp. 60, 61, 65-68.

expresses the prevailing attitude of mind in a characteristic sentence : " Infinite is the sweet variety that the Theorique of Musicke exerciseth the mind withall, as the contemplation of proportion, of Concords and Discords, diversity of Moods and Tones, infinitenesse of Invention, etc." [1] Many composers, treating music strictly as a science, occupied their time with mere experiments in complexity. Works were composed whose sole object seemed to be a multiplication of parts.[2] Conformity to rules was all-important. Vocal culture was limited almost entirely to the teaching of sight-singing and the " art of descant." Little or no attention was given to the manner of producing or modifying the quality of tones. Similarly instrumental virtuosity was rare, except among the highly trained professionals. The appeal to the emotions being a secondary matter, it was important only to " play the part correctly." In view of this formalizing tendency, it is surprising to find a real melodic beauty in many of the compositions of the period. Too often, however, it was lost under a mass of harmonic complexities and artificial embellishments.

But even at the beginning of the seventeenth century this rigidly formal theory of music was falling into disfavor. Thomas Campion, now known for his poetry rather than for his music, was one of the earliest to rebel. In the preface to his Ayres, 1601, he expressed himself very strongly against the old style of music, which he called " long, intricate, bated with fugue, chained with syncopation," and attacked in particular the " harsh and dull confused Fantasy, where in a multitude of Points the harmony is quite drowned." In consequence of

---

[1] *Compleat Gentleman*, p. 103.

[2] An " In Nomine of forty parts," written by Milton's father, is a famous example. See Aubrey, *Brief Lives* 2. 62 ; E. Philips, *Life*, pp. 352-353 ; and below, p. 12.

such views as these, the contrapuntal madrigals gradually lost their popularity. English music inclined towards the monodic style, thereby gaining in dramatic value, and preparing the way for recitative and opera. Polyphony became characteristic of instrumental rather than of vocal music, for it was found that the complicated harmonies which had been produced with difficulty by untrained voices became clear and pleasing when sounded by instruments, even in comparatively unskilled hands. The so-called " fancies " and " little consorts " for viols therefore grew to be the most popular instrumental forms, and on the vocal side the simple " ayres," with the accompaniment of the lute, took the place of the complicated madrigals.

The development of the monodic school resulted in a most intimate connection between English music and English poetry. In the time of the madrigals words had been of minor importance, often quite meaningless, and never more than mere doggerel. But in the new order of things there was no reason why the same man should write both text and music, for each of these now had a value of its own. The composers of " ayres " were only too glad to find material in the poetry of the day, and often added to its beauty by their settings. The poets, on the other hand, realized the advantages of music as an appeal to public favor, and were not slow to express their appreciation of the work of the composers.[1] Thus a mutually helpful intimacy arose. The music sometimes increased the effectiveness of the words ; the words often immortalized the music.[2]

[1] Harry Lawes, who seems to have been a great favorite, evoked commendatory verses not only from Milton, but from Waller and Herrick as well.

[2] Cf. for example the Milton-Lawes *Sweet Echo*. The import of this alliance between music and poetry is clearly revealed in Milton's own career, and it is therefore particularly to be emphasized.

It may be objected that in thus describing the English music of the seventeenth century I have neglected to take into account the hostile Puritan influences. These must, of course, be considered, yet they are by no means so important as is now generally supposed. Through the misstatements of historians, such as Ouseley and Hullah, the Puritan hostility to music has been grossly exaggerated, and their attitude entirely misrepresented. It is true that the Puritans often objected to sacred music. There are even traditions that some of the more fanatical showed their objections by destroying cathedral organs and choir-books.[1] But it cannot be proved that secular music was ever regarded with such disfavor. In fact, statistics show that throughout the period of Puritan supremacy music was composed, published, and performed as regularly as ever before.[2] In an anonymous *Short Treatise against Stage-plays* (1625) [3] we find the statement that " music is a cheerful recreation to the mind that hath been blunted with serious meditations." It is expressly mentioned among " holy and good recreations, both comfortable and profitable."

The attitude of William Prynne may well represent that of the average narrow-minded but educated Puritan. In his *Histriomastix* he attacks light music, it is true, but he begins the attack with the words " That Music of itself is lawful, useful, and commendable, no man, no Christian dares deny, since the Scriptures, Fathers, and generally all Christian, all Pagan authors extant, do with one consent aver it." [4]   As for the narrow-minded, un-

[1] See the citations in C. F. A. Williams' *Story of the Organ*, 1903, pp. 109-111.

[2] For these statistics, see Davey, pp. 274-275 ; *Oxford History of Music* 3. 208-209.

[3] Reprinted in the *Roxburgh Library*, 1869.

[4] *Histriomastix* 1. 5. 10.

educated type of Puritan, it is a well-known tradition that
the soldiers of the army went into battle singing Psalms.
Of the educated, broad-minded Puritans, Milton himself
belongs, of course, to the finest type.   But there were
others also who showed a very decided love for music.
Cromwell owned a valuable organ, kept a private musician, and gave " State concerts." [1]   Colonel Hutchinson,
the regicide, "could," according to his wife, " dance
admirably well," and " had a great love to music, and
often diverted himself with a viol, on which he played
masterly." [2]   Finally, as representing the uneducated but
liberal Puritan of later times, John Bunyan may be
cited.   His writings are full of the love of music, further
evidence of which is given by the well-known story of
the flute cut from the leg of a prison-chair.[3]

Puritan England, then, was by no means unmusical.
If anything, the attack upon ecclesiastical music strength-
ened the interest in secular music, and its popularity
increased rather than diminished.   It was only through
the degenerate taste of the Restoration period that
English music really suffered.   Of that period, however,
as having had no real influence on Milton, nothing need
be said here.

The seventeenth century, as a whole, represents the
climax and the succeeding decline of English music.   It
was a century which received the heritage of a musical
supremacy stretching as far back as the time of Henry VIII,
and reaching its highest level in the Elizabethan period.
As a result of this earlier supremacy, English music in
the seventeenth century commanded the widest popular
interest and enthusiasm ; and this enthusiasm was felt

---

[1] Firth, *Oliver Cromwell*, pp. 457-458.

[2] *Memoirs of the Life of Col. Hutchinson, by his Widow Lucy*,
H. G. Bohn, London, 1848, p. 22.

[3] See Davey, p. 267.

not so much for the emotional as for the formal aspect of music. Even the popular styles of composition were calculated to appeal to the intellect rather than to the feelings. The development of the monodic school, however, brought a more intelligent appreciation of the beauty of pure melody. Moreover the increasing importance of the words in vocal music led to a close alliance with the sister art of poetry, an alliance which showed its effects in the work of most of the greater musicians and poets of the day.[1]

Milton's environment, then, was distinctly musical. He lived at a time when the formalizing tendency of the Elizabethan period was still felt, but was mingled with a truer sense of proportion and a clearer recognition of values, the direct result of which was a close and mutually beneficial relationship between music and poetry.

[1] Cf. Milton's own reference to the " Sphere-born harmonious sisters, Voice and Verse," *S. M.* 2 ; and the sonnet *To Mr. H. Lawes.*

II

THE LIFE OF MILTON AS A MUSICIAN

An account of the music of Milton's time leads naturally to a consideration of the more vital influences in the poet's life—the influences of heredity and of peculiar environment.

Milton's father was a musician—no mere enthusiastic amateur, but a composer of real merit, " so eminently skilled . . . as to be ranked among the first masters of his time." [1]   Aubrey tells us that " he was an ingenious man, delighted in musique, composed many songs now in print, especially that of Oriana." [2]   Edward Philips, the poet's nephew, brings out the fact that the elder Milton, although a scrivener by trade, was not " wholly a slave to the world ; for he sometimes found vacant hours to the study (which he made his recreation) of the noble science of musick ", and that " for several songs of his composition . . . he gained the reputation of a considerable master in this most charming of all the liberal sciences." [3]

Aubrey and Philips both speak with admiration of an *In Nomine* of forty or possibly eighty parts, composed

[1] Hawkins 3. 368. Cf. Burney 3. 134, where the elder Milton is called " equal in science, if not genius, to the best musicians of his age." S. v. *Milton* in Grove's *Dict.*

[2] *Brief Lives* 2. 62.   The song " of Oriana " was a madrigal for six voices published in 1601 in a collection entitled " The Triumphs of Oriana " to which such eminent composers as Wilby, Morley, and Ellis Gibbons also contributed. Milton's song, No. xviii in the collection, was called " Fair Oriana in the Morn." The words are given by Todd, *Life*, 1809, p. 4, n.

[3] *Life* 352-353.

by Milton's father, for which he received a gold medal from " a Polish prince." [1]

Aside from such personal opinions, the ability of the elder Milton is clearly proved by his place as a composer in the best of the Elizabethan music-books.[2] A first-hand comparison of these works with the recognized master-pieces of the time shows Milton to have equalled the best of his contemporaries in contrapuntal skill, and to have been above the average in melodic inventiveness.

Milton's own estimate of his father as a musician is for us of the greatest interest. In his Latin Elegy *Ad Patrem* he builds up an elaborate defense of poetry. He urges his father's musical skill as one of the strongest arguments in favor of his own career as a poet, when he says :

[1] *Brief Lives* 2. 62 ; E. Philips, *Life* 352-353. For a definition of *In Nomine* see Hawkins 3. 280, n., and Grove's *Dict.* s. v. *In Nomine.*

[2] Four of his compositions appeared in Sir William Leighton's *Tears or Lamentations of a Sorrowful Soul*, 1614, namely *Thou God of Might*, four voices, printed in Burney 3. 139 ; *O Lord behold*, five voices, *O had I Wings*, five voices, printed in Hawkins 3. 369 ; *If that a Sinner's Sighs*, five voices. Byrd, Dowland, Wilby, and Coperario also contributed to this collection. The settings of the psalm tunes *York* and *Norwich*, appearing in Ravenscroft's *Psalter*, 1621, are by Milton's father. Hawkins (*Hist. of Music* 3. 367-368) says of "that common one called York tune" that "the tenor part of this tune is so well known, that within memory half the nurses in England were used to sing it by way of lullaby ; and the chimes of many country churches have played it six or eight times in four and twenty hours from time immemorial." A collection entitled *Tristitiae Remedium*, dated 1616 and probably edited by Thomas Myriell, contains six English and Latin motets by the elder Milton. Two of these, *When David heard* and *I am the Resurrection*, both for five voices, are printed in No. xxii, *Old English Edition*, from the British Museum *Add. Mss.* 29. 372-377. The other four, still in manuscript, are *O Woe is Me*, five voices, *Precamur sancte Domine*, *How doth the Holy City*, and *She weepeth continually*, all for six voices. Christ Church, Oxford, has manuscripts of *If ye love Me*, four voices, and five *Fancies* in five and six parts.

> Nor thou persist, I pray thee, still to slight
> The sacred Nine, and to imagine vain
> And useless, pow'rs, by whom inspir'd, thyself
> Art skilful to associate verse with airs
> Harmonious, and to give the human voice
> A thousand modulations, heir by right
> Indisputable of Arion's fame.
> Now say, what wonder is it, if a son
> Of thine delight in verse, if so conjoin'd
> In close affinity, we sympathize
> In social arts, and kindred studies sweet ?
> Such distribution of himself to us
> Was Phoebus' choice ; thou hast thy gift, and I
> Mine also, and between us we receive,
> Father and son, the whole inspiring God.[1]

With such a father to teach him the rudiments of the art it is only natural to suppose that the boy Milton was very early in life set to work at musical studies.[2] We can well imagine the musical atmosphere of the Milton household. There must have been an organ in the house, and probably there were other instruments as well, for the scrivener could afford certain luxuries. Possibly his musical friends assembled in his rooms at times. Some of the leading composers of the day may have been present at these informal gatherings. The great John Wilby, king of madrigal-writers, must have been at least an acquaintance of the Milton family.[3] Possibly the youthful genius, Thomas Ravenscroft, the famous Sir William Leighton, the modest but talented clergyman, Thomas

---

[1] *Ad Patrem* 56-66, Cowper's translation, pp. 61-62. Quoted in Latin below, Appendix I, p. 105.

[2] Aubrey says expressly, " His father instructed him " (*Brief Lives* 2. 67).

[3] His works appear in the same volumes as those of the elder Milton.

Myriell, visited the house at times.[1]   From such as these
the child Milton may have derived his first conceptions
of music—music of such excellence as to suggest to him
the song of the angels themselves.   We can imagine the
awe with which he listened as they tried over certain
madrigals or airs which they had just composed.   Later,
perhaps, when he had attained sufficiently " good skill,"
he was permitted to join in the music of these great men,
to sing a part at sight, or to play it upon the organ.

We are naturally curious to know what music-books
were read by the young poet in these first stages, and from
what sources, other than by word of mouth, he acquired
his fundamental knowledge.   It may be assumed that
any books in which the compositions of the elder Milton
appeared were always at hand; though, without any claim
upon personal interest, such a popular collection as the
Triumphs of Oriana must have occupied a prominent place
in every musical household.   Ravenscroft's *Psalter*, Leighton's *Tears or Lamentations* and Myriell's *Tristitiae Remedium* probably supplied the Milton family with sacred music.
Coperario's *Musical Banquet* and his *Funeral Tears for
the Earl of Devonshire* may have given the poet his first
acquaintance with the monodic style of composition.
On the side of theory, his earliest instruction may have
come from Morley's *Plain and Easy Introduction to Practical Music* ; and from this source he probably derived
his first conceptions of " proportion," of concord and
discord, and of " descant " or " measurable music."   But
he also showed very early a decided taste for the Greek
and Latin writers, and in their pages found much on
the subject of musical theory.   After once delving into
the mysticism of Pythagoras, as developed by Plato
and the later philosophers, it is hardly likely that the

---

[1] All these were editors of the elder Milton's compositions.

boy poet was satisfied with anything but the classic originals. Even Boethius and his jumble of supposedly scientific musical theory must have seemed tame in comparison with the great thoughts of the writers whom he imitated and attempted to expound.[1] The elder Milton encouraged this taste for the classics,[2] therefore it is very probable that, even before his University days, the boy had some knowledge of the ancient style of music.

At the time of his entrance into St. Paul's School, the young Milton is not only unusually proficient in his studies, but a musician of at least intelligence and appreciation, and probably of considerable skill. He plays the organ, and possibly other instruments as well.[3] He already knows something of theory and harmony. In St. Paul's Cathedral near by, he has an opportunity to hear the best sacred music of the day. Here he listens to the great sounds of the " pealing organ", something very different from the small instrument in his father's house.[4] The " service high and anthems clear," sung by the " full voiced quire," create in him a love of sacred music which continues throughout his life.

In his seventeenth year he enters Christ's College, Cambridge. By this time he has " acquired a proficiency in various languages, and . . . made a considerable progress in philosophy." [5] His musical horizon has also broadened. He is already formulating his own theory of cosmo-

[1] Aristoxenus, Aristides, Claudius Ptolemaeus, etc.

[2] *Ad Patrem* 78 ff.

[3] All biographers agree as to Milton's knowledge of the organ. Richardson, *Remarks on Milton*, p. v, adds the bass-viol. See also Todd, *Life*, p. 148, and *Earliest Life*, p. 21, quoted below, p. 53, n.

[4] John Tomkins was at that time organist at St. Paul's. The name of his brother, Thomas Tomkins, often appears in music-books with that of the elder Milton. It is likely that both were friends of the Milton family. *Dict. Nat. Biog.* s. v. *Tomkins*.

[5] *P. W.* 1. 254.

graphy, in which the mystic element of harmony assumes an important part.[1] It is a conception which is to remain with him throughout his life—the one fixed and unwavering point amid his constantly changing and discordant surroundings.

One of his first public exercises, written early in his university career, is an essay *On the Music of the Spheres*.[2] He shows in it a surprising knowledge of the Pythagorean system, and accuses Aristotle of misrepresenting its true meaning. His concluding words give the first indication of a thought expressed again and again in his later works: "If we bore pure, chaste, snow-clean hearts, as once Pythagoras did, then indeed our ears should resound with that sweetest music of the circling stars and be filled with it. Then all things should on the instant return as to that golden age. Then, free at last from our miseries, we should lead a life of ease, blessed and enviable even by the gods." [3] He introduces half jocular references to the same subject into his second epitaph on Hobson, the University Carrier.[4] His *Vacation Exercise* distinctly expresses his musical feeling,[5] and in another *Prolusion*, entitled *Mane citus lectum fuge*, there is a delicate appreciation of the music of Nature.[6] Evidently the youthful poet is beginning to look upon music more and more as a universal element. The ode *On the Morning of Christ's Nativity*, composed during Milton's sixth year at Cambridge, is full of music. It is the expression of a most remarkable instinct for effects of sound, which is here first shown to be characteristic of the poet.[7]

---

[1] This is indicated by various allusions in his earliest poems.

[2] See Appendix IV.

[3] Appendix IV, p. 136. Cf. *H*. 125-135 ; *S. M*. 17-28 ; *P. L*. 5. 144 ff.

[4] *U. C*. 2. 5-6.   [5] *V. Ex*. 33-38 ; 45-52 ; 62-64.

[6] Masson, *Life* 1. 304.   [7] Cf. below, pp. 90-92.

The spirit in which it is written is clearly illustrated by his letter to Diodati, in which he says, " We are engaged in singing the heavenly birth of the King of Peace . . . and the ethereal choirs of hymning angels." " You seem to be enjoying yourself rarely," he remarks, in the same letter. " Have you not music, the harp lightly touched by nimble hands, and the lute giving time to the fair ones as they dance in the old tapestried room ? " [1]

While at Cambridge Milton undoubtedly had a chance to learn something more of the art as well as of the theory of music. There was an organ at Christ's, and he was by this time well able to use it. John Hilton, later famous as a composer of airs, graduated Bachelor of Music at Trinity College in the second year of Milton's undergraduate life, and it is likely that he took an interest in the music of a young man whose father was so well-known and highly honored in his own field. That Milton took any active part in the musical affairs of the University, however, cannot be proved. In his later years he showed some interest in the university theatricals, but in a spirit more of contempt than of admiration.[2]

With his retirement to Horton, the poet devoted himself with increased zeal to the study of the classics. His father's influence sustained his interest in music, and he probably completed at this time his reading of the Greek writers on theory. He tells us, also, that he often went to London to learn " something new in mathematics or music." [3] The combination is a natural one. To Milton the mathematical or formal side of music always appealed through its exactness and strict adherence to law. He was fond of dwelling upon the " numbers " and the " measure " of music.[4] The visits to town do not necessarily

---

[1] *E.* 6. 81-85 ; 37-40. Masson's translation, *Life* 1. 227.
[2] Cf. *P. W.* 3. 114-115, and Masson, *Life* 1. 220 ff.   [3] *P. W.* 1. 255.
[4] *P. L.* 3. 38 ; 580 ; 5. 150 ; *P. R.* 1. 170 ; 4. 255 ; *A.* 71.

indicate regular lessons. The poet was in the habit of picking up books of all kinds when he had the opportunity, and he probably took as much interest in a new collection of airs or of organ pieces as in volumes of a more serious nature. It may also be suggested that he sometimes listened, when he had the opportunity, to public performances of good music, just as he occasionally patronized the theatre. We can imagine the young poet meeting on these occasions with a small circle of musical friends, either for the practice or the enjoyment of the art. It is to be assumed that the acquaintance of Milton with the composer Harry Lawes dated from the early part of the Horton period. Possibly Lawes was Milton's music teacher, although there is no real evidence to prove that such a relation existed between them. The musician was fourteen years older than the poet, yet a close friendship, founded upon mutual admiration, sprang up between them. When Lawes was requested to furnish a masque in honor of the aged Countess of Derby, he naturally turned to Milton for the words, himself supplied the music, and the result was the *Arcades*.[1] Here again the young Milton employed his conception of the music of the spheres with high poetic effect, and in so doing again clearly reflected the influence of the Greek theory of music.[2]

In the year following the production of *Arcades* Milton and Lawes once more combined their talents to produce a masque, this time the *Comus*. Lawes himself played a part, and Milton took advantage of this chance to introduce various subtle flatteries of his friend's musical ability.[3]

---

[1] The question whether Milton's part in the *Arcades* and *Comus* was due to Lawes has been much discussed. After all, it matters little whether both were engaged independently, or the one at the request of the other.

[2] Cf. *A.* 62-78, and Appendix I, p. 107.

[3] Cf. *C.* 494-496 ; 86-88, and see Appendix II, pp. 124-127.

In 1637 Lawes was permitted by Milton to publish the poem, although the author's name was concealed. The high esteem in which the musician held the attainment of his young friend is shown by his dedicatory epistle to Lord Brackley, in which he calls the masque " so lovely, and so much desired that the often copying of it hath tired my pen to give my several friends satisfaction, and brought me to a necessity of producing it to the public view." Eight years later Milton returned the compliment with a sonnet in praise of Lawes' music, which, in 1648, was prefixed, with other tributes of a similar nature, to the edition of his *Choice Psalms*. Whether or not we agree with the seemingly extravagant laudations of this sonnet, the sincerity of Milton's opinion cannot be doubted.[1]

One more event is to be noted in the friendship of John Milton and Harry Lawes. When, in 1638, the poet planned a journey to France and Italy, he was spared the trouble of securing a passport in the regular fashion, for Lawes used his influence to procure for him a " letter from my Lord Warden of the Cinque Ports under his hand and seal, which," he said, " will be a sufficient warrant to justify your going out of the King's dominions." [2]

In Italy Milton enters upon a new world of literature, science, art, and music. He visits the aged, blind Galileo, and possibly derives from him fresh hints regarding the mathematics of music, in which the astronomer has been particularly interested.[3] He is received with open arms

---

[1] See the notes in Appendix II, pp. 124-128.

[2] See the letter from Henry Lawes, Masson, *Life* 1. 736.

[3] " From his father, who was an exquisite performer on the lute, he [Galileo] learnt both the theory and practice of music with such success that he is said to have excelled him in charm of style and delicacy of touch. He was taught by his father to

by the Florentine scholars, and made a member of the Academy of the Svogliati. Here he meets the most cultured gentlemen of the city. He takes part in the regular club meetings, reading his Latin hexameters, which are enthusiastically applauded. He enters into scholarly discussions, some of which may even deal with his favorite theory of music.[1]

He continues his journey to Rome, where a similar reception awaits him. The great Cardinal Francesco Barberini, well-known as a patron of music, becomes his personal friend. He invites him to a magnificent "musical entertainment" at his palace, and receives him in person at the door.[2]

It was probably on this occasion that Milton for the first time heard the famous singer, Leonora Baroni. Accompanied by her mother and her sister on theorbo and lute, she interpreted in an entrancing manner the Italian music of the time. Leonora's singing was among the few impressions of this journey which Milton thought worth recording in verse. He addressed three extravagant Latin epigrams to her. She brought again to his mind the celestial harmony, which she of all mortals seemed fit to reproduce.[3] Milton's epigrams are conventional in their extravagance ; he probably would not have wished

---

play on the organ and on other instruments ; but the lute was his favorite instrument. He found it a pleasure in youth, and a solace in the last days of his life, when blindness was added to his other sorrows."—*The Private Life of Galileo* (anonymous), p. 3. See also J. J. Fatier, *Galileo, his Life and Work*, p. 6 ; Ludwig Pilgrim, *Galilei*, p. 6.

[1] A sentence in Carlo Dati's letter to Milton (1639) suggests this idea, when he refers to the poet as one " who, with astronomy as his guide, hears the harmonious sounds of the celestial spheres." —Masson, *Life* 1. 785.

[2] See Milton's letter to Lucas Holstenius, *P. W.* 3. 499.

[3] Cf. the three epigrams, and the notes in Appendix III.

his sentiments to be taken literally. Yet he had, no doubt, a sincere admiration for her musical talent, and expressed it in the poetical terms current at the time.[1]

At this time, also, he may have heard the organ-playing of Frescobaldi, the most famous performer of the day on that instrument.[2] His mastery of fugue and his skill in improvising must have impressed Milton deeply. We find distinct descriptions of such a type of musician in his later writings.[3]

It is hardly likely that Milton at this time came in contact with Cardinal Barberini's favorite, the musician Giovanni Battista Doni, who was then absent from Rome. But when Milton visited Florence a second time, they must certainly have met. Doni's name occurs in the minutes of a meeting of the Svogliati, and he is reported to have " read a scene from his Tragedy ", while Milton's share in the program consisted of " various Latin poems."[4] Doni was not only an accomplished performer, but a composer of some merit and a distinguished writer on theory,[5] and we are justified in thinking that he did

---

[1] A. Ademollo, in his pamphlet *La Leonora di Milton e di Clemente IX.*, Ed. Ricordi, no. 50281, takes it for granted that Milton was in love with Leonora. Cf. also W. Hayley's note to the first epigram in his edition of Cowper's translations of Milton, 1808. There is no reason for believing that Milton regarded Leonora with personal affection, or that she was the mysterious lady of the Italian sonnets.

[2] A. G. Ritter, *Zur Geschichte des Orgelspiels*, p. 207, in speaking of the complex character of Frescobaldi's organ music, says : " Er ist unter allen Orgelspielern, die je gelebt haben, der einzige, der solche Aufgaben denken und lösen konnte. Keine Schule hat ihm diese Fähigkeit beigebracht ; sie war bei ihm ein Wiegengeschenk, wie es die Natur jeweilig dem einzelnen mit auf den Weg gibt, zu Gunsten, oder zu Ungunsten, stets aber zu kennzeichnender Ausprägung der Individualität."

[3] Cf. *P. L.* 11. 561—563.

[4] See Stern, *Milton und seine Zeit*, vol. 2, Appendix 2.

[5] See Hawkins 4. 190-203.

much to increase Milton's respect for contemporary Italian music.[1]

Before returning home, Milton sent from Venice a number of books which he had collected in his travels, "particularly," as Edward Philips tells us, " a chest or two of choice music books of the best masters flourishing about that time in Italy—namely, Luca Marenz(i)o, Monte Verde, Horatio Vecchi, Cif(r)a, the Prince of Venosa, and several others."[2] We may well imagine how the poet on his return exhibited these newly-found treasures to his aged father and to his interested friend Harry Lawes. There is no reason to believe that his intimacy with the latter ceased even with the outbreak of the Civil War.[3]

During the winter of 1639—40, Milton undertook the education of his two little nephews, Edward and John Philips. He made music an important part of his instruction. Aubrey says, "He made his nephews songsters, and sing from the time they were with him."[4] The boys evidently acquired considerable skill and taste in music, for later in life they were in close touch with the best musical circles in London.[5]

It was Milton's sincere conviction that music should form an important part in any scheme of education. He

[1] Milton speaks of Doni in a letter to Holstenius, March 30, 1639, *P. W.* 3. 499. Athanasius Kircher, another favorite of Cardinal Barberini, was also in Rome at this time, and associated with Doni. His *Musurgia Universalis*, published in 1650, contains some strikingly Miltonic ideas. Milton may well have seen parts of the work in manuscript.

[2] Philips, *Life*, p. 361.

[3] Cf. the laudatory sonnet, published, 1648, in a volume dedicated to the captive king.

[4] *Brief Lives* 2. 64.

[5] Godwin emphasizes the musical ability of both brothers. Cf. *Lives of Edward and John Philips*, pp. 150, 327.

wrote in his *Tractate of Education*, in 1644, that in the ideal academy of learning, the intervals " before meat " should be taken up with " the solemn and divine harmonies of music, heard or learned, either whilst the skilful organist plies his grave and fancied descant in lofty fugues, or the whole symphony with artful and unimaginable touches adorn and grace the well-studied chords of some choice composer ; sometimes the lute or soft organ-stop waiting on elegant voices, either to religious, martial, or civil ditties, which, if wise men and prophets be not extremely out, have a great power over dispositions and manners, to smooth and make them gentle from rustic harshness and distempered passions. The like also would not be inexpedient after meat, to assist and cherish nature in her first concoction, and send their minds back to study in good tune and satisfaction." [1]

But Milton's own mind can scarcely have been " in good tune " at this time. His marriage with Mary Powell in 1643 had proved unhappy. His soul failed to find the " harmony " which it demanded, and while it is possible that no violent discords arose, yet Milton's married life was anything but an "undisturbed song of pure concent." In the midst of the doubts brought upon him by the desertion of his wife, he began to write those pamphlets on the divorce question which raised a discordant uproar throughout all England. [2]

But even though the poet failed to discover the ideal harmony which he sought, the actual harmonies of music must have continued to remain a comfort and a pleasure to him. He still had his pupils, his songs, and his organ. There is a passage in the *Areopagitica* (1644) showing how

---

[1] *P. W.* 3. 476. See Appendix I, p. 111.

[2] *The Doctrine and Discipline of Divorce*, 1643 ; *The Judgement of Martin Bucer concerning Divorce*, 1644 ; *Tetrachordon*, 1644-5 ; *Colasterion*, 1645. Cf. also Sonnets 11 and 12, 1645.

his mind turned most naturally to music as analogous to literature, when he speaks contemptuously of licensing musical instruments in the same manner in which books are to be licensed.[1]

With the return of his wife and the removal to Barbican (1645) a more peaceful period began. The town house of the Earl of Bridgewater was near by, and possibly Milton renewed his acquaintance with the Lady Alice and Mr. Thomas Egerton, who had taken part in the *Comus* more than ten years before. Harry Lawes was still intimate with both the Egerton and the Milton families, and his visits to Barbican must have been frequent. It was at this time (Feb. 9, 1645—6) that Milton wrote his extravagant sonnet in praise of Lawes.[2] Early in the same year the first edition of his poems was published.[3] The title-page reads, " Poems of Mr. John Milton, both English and Latin, compos'd at several times . . . The Songs were set in musick by Mr. Henry Lawes." From this Masson argues that Lawes set music to other works of Milton besides the *Arcades* and *Comus*.[4] It is thus evident that there was no break in the friendship between the musician and the poet, and the intimacy probably continued until Lawes' death in 1662.

From this time on to the end of Milton's life, the record of his musical interests must be gathered almost entirely from the allusions in his works. Of actual facts few are recorded. His father, the aged musician-scrivener, died in 1647. Five years later, Milton's eyes, long tried by excessive study and the demands of public work, failed completely. Is it not likely that with the beginning of Milton's blindness his sense for sound increased ? Nature is commonly credited with atoning in some degree for the afflictions visited upon men. Certainly in his later

---

[1] *P. W.* 2. 73. See Appendix I, p. 112.   [2] See above, p. 20.
[3] Jan. 2, 1645-6.   [4] Masson, *Life* 3. 464.

poetical works Milton shows a decided preference for the description of audible impressions, a love of the sounds in Nature rather than its visible beauties, a sensitiveness of hearing rather than of sight.[1] This peculiar delight in sounds had, it is true, been characteristic of Milton all through his life, yet there can be no doubt that it increased perceptibly and found a more decided expression in his writings after his blindness came upon him.[2]

The lines of *Paradise Lost* are full of musical reminiscences. Echoes of madrigals and anthems heard long ago resound in the song of the angel choirs. Real figures of the past, Leonora singing at Rome, Frescobaldi playing the organ, are reflected again in visionary, supernatural forms. All the musical elements of the pagan cosmology are refashioned into his Christian idea of heaven, where celestial melodies, arising from the very motion of the spheres, resound unceasingly. The poet's unquenchable desire for harmony is the dominant motive. It is a longing which in his earthly experience has never been satisfied, a fixed idea which has possessed him throughout his life. In the face of the constant changes of his condition, of the jangle and discord of strife and quarrel ever grating upon his delicate sensibilities, this one purpose has remained fixed.[3] He has failed to discover a religious, a political, or even a domestic harmony which could satisfy his soul. But from his actual experience, his knowledge of natural laws, he builds up a strong faith

---

[1] Cf. especially the opening of the Third Book of *Paradise Lost*, quoted in part below, Appendix I, pp. 114-115.

[2] Richardson tells an interesting story illustrating Milton's substitution of hearing for sight. " Milton, hearing a lady sing finely, ' Now will I swear,' says he, ' this lady is handsome.' His ears now were eyes to him." Richardson, p. vi.

[3] " Many of his choicest years of life were employed in wrangling, and receiving and racquetting back reproach, accusation, and sarcasm . . . Only Musick he enjoyed."—Richardson, pp. cii, ciii.

in a complete spiritual harmony which must exist for him somewhere in the future, and which at present can be but a mystical ideal.

Of the last years of the poet's life few details are known. His third wife, Elizabeth Minshull, who was with him up to the time of his death, is described by Aubrey as " a gent. person, a peaceful and agreeable humor." [1] There is a tradition that she could sing, and that Milton told her playfully that she had a good voice but no ear.[2] Aubrey tells us that " he had an organ in his house ; he played on that most."[3] Probably it had been the property of his father before him. The little gatherings of musical friends evidently still continued. Such a one is indicated in the sonnet *To Mr. Lawrence* (1656–60) in which the chief of the pleasures described is

> To hear the lute well touched, or artful voice
> Warble immortal notes and Tuscan air.[4]

When his final illness set in, it was by his music that he supported his spirits. " He would be cheerful even in his gout fits, and sing," [5] not the psalms or the doleful chants of a dying man, I take it, but the fresh, undismayed songs of one in whose soul the spirit of harmony was as strong as ever.

---

[1] *Brief Lives* 2. 65. [2] Masson, *Life* 6. 477.
[3] *Brief Lives* 2. 67. Cf. also Richardson, p. v., and Toland, *Life* 138 ; 139.
[4] *S.* 20. 11-12. [5] Aubrey, *Brief Lives* 2. 67.

III

MILTON AND THE ART OF MUSIC

That Milton possessed a thorough knowledge of the art of music is affirmed by all his biographers. His works, moreover, are full of technical allusions whose significance cannot be overlooked. A study of these sources of information shows him to have been an active musician both in practice and in theory—playing and singing himself, listening to concerts, taking a lively interest in the instruments, the performances, and the compositions of his day, instructing his pupils in music, possibly even experimenting at times with compositions of his own.[1] The depth of his musical culture and the extent of his experience in the art at once suggest certain definite and interesting inquiries. What was the measure of his abilities ? What were his tastes ? Were his sympathies with the music of his own time, or with that of the past ? In what way did his mental life in general affect his attitude towards so definite and concrete a subject ?

As to the poet's musical ability, it is easy to judge. He had, first and foremost, a thorough knowledge of the organ. It was, according to all biographers, his favorite instrument, a preference easily inferred from his frequent allusions to the organ, both in his poetry and in his prose. He not only discusses it with intimate knowledge, but treats it with evident personal affection as well. It is the only musical instrument mentioned in his *Common-*

---

[1] Cf. Aubrey, *Brief Lives* 2. 64 ; 67 ; Richardson, p. ii ; v ; ciii ; Toland, *Life*, p. 138 ; Todd, *Life*, pp. 148, 149 ; *P. W.* 1. 255 ; and see above, pp. 14, 16, 18, 21, 22, 23.

place Book.[1] He shows an interest not only in the sounds, but in the structure of the instrument. At one time he tells us how

> in an organ, from one blast of wind,
> To many a row of pipes the sound-board breathes.[2]

The statement is accurate, but by no means obvious to one who is not a musician.[3] At other times he is careful to dwell upon the *blowing* of the organ—to speak of it as a *wind-instrument.*[4] When, in his *Second Defence of the People of England*, Milton declares that he " can hardly refrain from assuming a more lofty and swelling tone," [5] the expression inevitably suggests the poet sitting at his organ, improvising in simple, harmonious measures, but now and then tempted to draw out a stop, and thunder his indignation *fortissimo.*

Naturally he idealizes his favorite instrument. To him it is the most fitting expression of the sublime in Nature. When the spheres add their music to that of the angel choirs in praise of the birth of the Savior, " the bass of Heaven's deep organ " is the foundation of the universal harmony.[6] On the day of rest, " not in silence holy kept," the music of Heaven includes " all organs of sweet

---

[1] Under the heading *De Musica* the following item is included : " Organa primum in Gallia, Les Ambassadeurs de Constantin emperour Grec apportérent à roy Pepin des Orgues, qu'on n'avoit pas encore veuës en France.'—Girard, *Hist. France* 1. 3, p. 138." (C. F. A. Williams, *Story of the Organ*, pp. 27-28, states that " the emperor Copronymus VI of Constantinople sent an organ as a present to Pepin, the father of Charlemagne, in A. D. 757, which was placed in the church of St. Corneille at Campiagne, there being no organs in France at the time.")

[2] *P. L.* 1. 708-709.

[3] See the explanation in Keightley, *Life*, p. 433, and the diagram in C. F. A. Williams, *Story of the Organ*, p. 21. Cf. also Kircher, *Mus. Univ.* 6. 3.

[4] *Il P.* 161 ; *H.* 130.   [5] *P. W.* 1. 219.   [6] *H.* 130.

stop." [1]   Adam's vision of the music of the sons of Jubal
has for its central figure an organist whose

> volant touch
> Instinct through all proportions low and high
> Fled and pursued transverse the resonant fugue.[2]

In his theory of education Milton lays great stress
upon music, and it is the organ accompanying the voice
which is to exercise its " power over dispositions and
manners, to smooth and make them gentle from rustic
harshness and distempered passions." [3]   Only once does
Milton speak slightingly of the organ.   In this single
instance, however,[4] he attacks the misuse of the organ in
the Chapel Royal, rather than the organ itself.   Even
though he may have appreciated the technical skill
required for " the masterful running over many chords
and divisions," [5] he was not in sympathy with the florid
and frivolous compositions which the King's musicians
dignified with the name of " sacred music." [6]   In any
case, as Milton is writing here for his party rather than for
himself, and in the approved polemic style of the time,
he may well be attacking publicly that which his private
judgment might have excused.

The organ, then, must be considered Milton's own instrument, the one which he knew best and loved most,
the one which earliest gave him his introduction to the

[1] *P. L.* 7. 596.   The reference may, however, apply merely to
wind instruments in general. See Glossary.

[2] *P. L.* 11. 561-563.   The organist here is an elaboration of the
hint contained in Gen. 4. 21. See below, Appendix I, p. 121.

[3] *Tractate on Education*, *P. W.* 3. 476. See below, Appendix I,
pp. 111-112.

[4] *Eikonoklastes*, *P. W.* 1. 461.

[5] *P. W.* 3. 62.

[6] Cf. the " difficult passages " cited by Burney 3. 115-117 ;
and cf. Hawkins 3. 461-464.

mysteries of the art,[1] and satisfied his latest desires for the music of this earth,[2] the one which permitted the closest technical study and demanded the most sublime idealization. No other instrument is so important as the organ in a consideration of Milton's interest in music.

Some of his biographers record that he played the bass viol.[3] There is no reason to doubt the statement, for the ability to perform on some stringed instrument was almost indispensable to the training of a gentleman. But Milton could never have loved the ponderous and dull-toned bass viol as he did the versatile, endlessly complex organ.[4] In his works there are but two passing references to viols in general,[5] a fact which, in itself, makes any personal liking for the instrument extremely doubtful.

The lute, the most popular instrument of Milton's day, seems to have lent itself only to a conventional use by the poet. He recognizes its value as an instrument of accompaniment to the voice, and mentions it in no other connection. He admires the softness and delicacy of its sound.[6] When the famous singer, Leonora Baroni, was accompanied by her mother, Ariana, on the lute, he was enchanted with the effect.[7] His musical friend, Harry Lawes, was a skilled lutenist. In his later years, when the poet attended such congenial gatherings as he describes in his sonnet *To Mr. Lawrence,* one of his chief pleasures was " to hear the lute well-touched." [8] The

[1] Cf. Aubrey, *Brief Lives* 2. 67.

[2] Cf. Richardson, p. v., and Toland, *Life,* p. 138.

[3] Richardson, p. v ; Todd, *Life,* p. 149 ; *Earliest Life,* p. 21.

[4] Of course the bass viol of Milton's day must not be confused with the modern instrument. See Glossary, and Kircher, *Mus. Univ.* 6. 1.

[5] *P.* 28 ; *P. W.* 2. 73.

[6] *P.* 28 ; *P. W.* 3. 476.

[7] *Ad Leonoram* 2. 6.

[8] *S.* 20. 11. Cf. also *P. L.* 5. 151 ; *C.* 478 ; *P. W.* 2. 73.

poet's interest in the lute was real in one way at least.
It evidently was to him the contemporary representative
of the ancient lyre. Here the classic spirit of the poet
again asserts itself. The lute was less interesting to Milton as the favorite instrument of polite society than
when he saw in it the descendant and true copy of the
primitive combination of thongs and tortoise-shell to
which immortal strains were sung. Reproducing those
ancient sounds as closely as possible, the lute acquired a
new significance. The poet evidently considered the
terms " lyre " and " lute " as almost synonymous. He
speaks calmly of " Apollo's lute," when addressing
Englishmen in English surroundings,[1] and conversely,
when writing Latin epigrams to Leonora, her mother's
lute becomes a " lyra."[2]

The classic influences suggested by Milton's use of the
lute are evident in his treatment of other instruments also.
He alludes often to the lyre, for it is the conventional
stringed instrument of pagan mythology, and it is only
natural that these allusions should occur in the Latin
poems.[3] Here he uses not only the general term *lyra*,[4]
which could be applied to any member of the family, but
the technical names of particular kinds of lyres as well.
Some of these names he may have taken directly from
classic poetry, almost as if they were formulas to fit certain situations. At times we are tempted to believe that
the metre of the line determined the name of the instrument. Yet it would be unfair to say that these
classic names were meaningless to him, that they were

---

[1] *C.* 478.

[2] *Ad Leonoram* 2. 6.

[3] The only mention of the lyre in the English works is a conventional reference to the " Orphean lyre," *P. L.* 3. 17.

[4] *Epit.* 218 ; *Ad Leonoram* 2. 6. Cf. the description in Kircher,
Mus. Univ. 2. 6.

mere words, fit only to give a pleasant sound to a line. Even though he could not have been familiar with the actual sounds of the various ancient lyres, he must have had some conception of their quality through his knowledge of the stringed instruments of his own day, and he must have been aware of differences in structure from his reading of ancient authors. So, when he makes the *cithara* the instrument of Apollo,[1] or applies it to a pagan conception of the celestial music,[2] he does so in the full consciousness that he is speaking of the largest and most highly developed member of the lyre family.[3] When the playing of Orpheus, however, is mentioned,[4] his instrument is the *barbitos*—a lyre of long and narrow shape having many strings.[5] The *chelys*, a small, primitive lyre, dominates a most charming picture of a festal dance, at an English country-house in contemporary setting, but in the classic spirit.[6] Here the daintiness of the instrument, the rhythmic strokes of the plectrum, and the swift movements of the dancing maidens, all appeal equally to his poetic fancy.[7] In a very different spirit he refers to the *pecten*,[8] as the conventional accompaniment of a bard's chanting.

[1] *Ad Mansum* 63.   [2] *Ad Patrem* 54.

[3] The expression " citharaeque sciens," *Epit.* 89, is, as Todd notes, a mere echo of Horace, *Od.* 3. 9. 9. Cf. also Virg. *Aen.* 6. 120.

[4] *E.* 6. 37. See also *Ad Rousium* 9.

[5] Cf. Horace, *Od.* 1. 32. 3 ; 3. 26. 3 ; Martianus Capella, *De Nupt. Phil.* 1. 36.

[6] *E.* 6. 38-46.

[7] For classic uses of the *chelys* cf. Martianus Capella, *De Nupt. Phil.* 1. 36 ; Pompon. *Apud Terentian. de Metr.* 2137. Kircher, *Mus. Univ.* 2. 4. 1, calls the *chelys* that instrument " quam vulgo viola gamba vocant," a definition which would have little significance in the present instance.

[8] *Ad Rousium* 10. The *pecten* is literally the plectrum, but used by synechdoche for the lyre itself. Cf. Ovid, *Fast.* 2. 121 : " Dum canimus sacras alterno pectine nonas."

Milton's use of these classic names, therefore, is by no means blind or meaningless. While it is impossible, in most cases, to interpret his conception accurately, it is evident enough that he did possess a clear conception of each. Milton was too sincere to assume distinctions which were not real.

The function of the lyre in the Latin poems is supplied by the harp in the English works. Here again the poet treats of an instrument the art of playing which may be quite unknown to him, but of whose quality of sound he has, nevertheless, a distinct conception. Just as the lyre is the instrument of Apollo, of Orpheus, and of departed spirits, so the harp is the instrument of the celestial choirs.[1] Like the lute and the lyre, it is used merely to accompany the voice. But whereas Milton's treatment of the lute and the lyre is affected by classical influences, his conception of the harp is derived from Scripture. This is quite in accord with the habits of the poet. As most of his English poetry employs a Christian setting, we should expect to find his musical references taken from Christian sources. Thus the harp figures largely in Milton's descriptions of Heaven. Even the fallen angels

> sing
> With notes angelical to many a harp
> Their own heroic deeds.[2]

The nature of the celestial music is elaborately set forth in the account of the creation: each day is begun with the sound of harps and of celestial voices joined in songs of adoration.[3] At the birth of the Savior

[1] A reference to the " harp of Orpheus," *P. W.* 3. 467, seems to show that the terms lyre and harp are synonymous to Milton. Cf. *P. L.* 7. 36-37. The " harp and organ " of Genesis 4. 21 are in the Vulgate " cithara et organo."

[2] *P. L.* 2. 547-549.

[3] *P. L.* 7. 258-259 ; 449-450 ; 558-560 ; 594-595. Cf. also *P. L.* 3. 365-369.

The helmèd Cherubim
And sworded Seraphim
Are seen in glittering ranks with wings displayed,
Harping in loud and solemn quire.[1]

When the harp is described as a part of the music of mortals, it is, as a rule, the conventional intrument of the bard, again resembling, in this respect, the lyre of classic poetry.[2]   Milton " sets " his harp " to notes of saddest woe " when preparing to write of the Passion.[3]   When glorifying the Son of God in triumphant measures, he adds, "and never shall my harp thy praise forget."[4]   In the orisons of Adam and Eve the suggestion of a possible accompaniment of " lute or harp " is rejected without hesitation.[5]   The " harp and organ " of the sons of Jubal is, of course, taken directly from Gen. 4. 21.[6]   When the tempted Christ refers with pride to " our Hebrew songs and harps," [7] he is using a mere conventional formula for sacred poetry.

Milton's use of the harp, therefore, is to a great extent figurative, and the large number of allusions occurring throughout his works is not indicative of a real preference. Strictly speaking, the element of personal affection enters alone into Milton's treatment of the organ.   In the case of practically all other instruments his language suggests conventionality, sometimes even direct imitation.

The trumpet occurs even more often than the harp— eighteen times in the English poems, nine times in the prose, with several additional references in the Latin Poems.[8]   It is, of course, likewise a conventional instru-

---

[1] *H*. 112 ff.   Cf. *S. M*. 12-13 ; and *P. W*. 2. 479.
[2] There is also, naturally, a certain dependence on Scriptural usage. Cf. the description of Hebrew harps in Kircher, *Mus. Univ*. 2. 4. 1.
[3] *P*. 9.   [4] *P. L*. 3. 414-415.   [5] *P. L*. 5. 151.   [6] *P. L*. 11. 560.
[7] *P. R*. 4. 336.   [8] See references in the Glossary.

ment of the Bible,[1] and Milton adapts it without hesitation to the music of his celestial choirs.[2]   But there is
one distinct feature in Milton's use of the trumpet which
is not only Biblical but classical as well : he treats the
instrument, not as a part of a mixed band or orchestra,
but as a signal, a sound of acclaim, or a mere noise.   This
is precisely the part played by the trumpet in the Greek
music.   Strictly speaking, it had no place whatever in the
real instrumental music, which consisted entirely of flutes
and strings.   It merely gave the signal or the inspiration
for battle, and, as such, its sound excited on the one hand
terror, and, on the other, ferocity rather than pleasure.
But in Milton's own time the trumpet had become, to
some extent, an instrument of harmony in a band.[3]   It
is worth noting, therefore, that Milton remains faithful to
classical tradition in the face of contemporary usage.

He is fond of alluding to the " trump of doom," to the
warning of its sound, to its loudness and its terrible
effect.[4]   At times, however, it is the instrument of joy
and of acclamation, as when the

> bright Seraphim in burning row
> Their loud uplifted angel-trumpets blow.[5]

[1] Cf. I. Chronicles 13. 8 ; 15. 24 ; II. Chronicles 5. 12 ; 29. 27 ;
Ps. 81. 3 ; 98. 6 ; Numbers 10 ; 29 ; Joshua 6. 4 ; Judges 7. 16 ;
Levit. 23.24 ; Ezek 7. 14 ; 33. 3 ; Joel 2. 1 ; Rev. 8 ; 9. 11. Cf.
the descriptions of trumpets, flutes, etc., in Kircher, *Mus. Univ.* 2.
4. 3 ; 6. 2. 2.

[2] *P. L.* 1. 754 ; 2. 514-515 ; 6. 59-60 ; 203-204 ; 526 ; 11. 72-74 ;
S. M. 10-11.

[3] Cf. Whitelocke, *Memorials,* London, 1732, p. 20, and the stage
directions for music in old plays. Henry VIII's band contained
fourteen trumpets and ten trombones. Queen Elizabeth used ten
trumpets and six trombones in the court orchestra. Monteverde
arranged his orchestration for eight trumpets. Grove's *Dict.* s. v.
trumpet ; Eichhorn, *Die Trompete in alter und neuer Zeit, passim.*

[4] Cf. *H.* 156 ; *P. L.* 1. 532 ; 754 ; 6. 59-60 ; *P. R.* 1. 19 ; *P. W.* 2.
474 ; 3. 70.   [5] *S. M.* 10-11.

But there is no hint, even here, of any harmony other than a strict unison. Lastly, the trumpet often represents to Milton mere noise. In one instance, at least, he seems to treat it with contempt.[1]

But the most striking classical influences on Milton's use of instrumental music appear in his love of the pastoral pipe and reed. Here at times he actually speaks, as it were, in the person of an ancient pastoral poet. Not only does he picture himself as a shepherd in *Lycidas* and the *Epitaphium Damonis*, but others of his works, particularly the *Arcades* and the *Comus*, are full of pastoral elements ; thus he seems to have preferred the pipe and the reed to other conventional instruments such as the syrinx or the lyre. Moreover, the sounds of these instruments of antiquity he realized through the flutes and the organ-pipes of his own time. We may therefore believe that in his allusions to the pipe and reed Milton is not simply following the time-honored conventions of pastoral poetry. This is only partly true. For his ear is so sensitive, and his love of music so constant that even these conventional instruments suggest to his imagination distinct tone and quality.

[1] *P. W.* 1. 232. He first quotes the author of *The Royal Blood crying to Heaven for vengeance on the English Parricides* to the effect that " after this proaemium, Salmasius will make the trumpet blow a deadly blast." Milton's bitterly satirical comment is as follows : " You announce a new kind of harmony, for to the terrors of that loud-sounding instrument no symphony bears so close a resemblance as that which is produced by accumulated flatulency. But I advise Salmasius not to raise the notes of this trumpet to too high a pitch, for, the louder the tones, the more he will expose himself to a slap on the chops ; which, while both his cheeks ring, will give a delightful flow to his well-proportioned melodies." These words, however, cannot be considered indicative of Milton's better convictions or taste. They are merely another example of conventional polemic style. Cf. *P.W.* 1. 461. The allusion to " Cremona's trump," *P.* 26, may also be considered as contemptuous. See G.

In speaking of the pipe he dwells upon its softness, its smoothness, its solemnity of tone.[1] At times he finds in it the expression of a sportive mood, typical of rural merriment,[2] but on the whole he prefers its gentler, quieter sounds. As he pictures himself in the Christian poems singing to the harp, so in his pastorals he becomes a piping shepherd.[3]

One point is clearly illustrated by Milton's general attitude toward instrumental music. He always shows a thorough knowledge of the quality and effect of tones with which he deals. Even when he is unable to play an instrument, or has never, with bodily ear, heard its actual sound, he gains a clear conception of its quality either by hearsay or by applying his imagination to the effects of some contemporary instrument of a similar character ; and when he has thus acquired a distinct conception, there is never any hesitation or inconsistency in his treatment of a particular instrument. The quality of its tone in his mind is distinct and unchanging ; it has for him a fixed and definite function ; this he carefully and distinctly affirms. Certain instruments fit certain situations—produce certain effects. They cannot be in-

[1] *C.* 86-87 ; *P. L.* 1. 561 ; 7. 595.

[2] *C.* 173 ; 823 ; *Il P.* 126.

[3] It is unnecessary to point out the many classical echoes in Milton's allusions to the pipe and reed. They may be found in the best editions of his works. His use of the " oat ", *L.* 33 ; 88 ; *C.* 345, copies the *avena* of Virgil and Ovid, *Ecl.* 1. 2 ; *Met.* 2. 677 ; 8. 191. The *cicuta* of *Epit. Dam.* 135 is also an example of classic usage, representing the flute, pipe, or reed. When Milton speaks of " vocal reeds," in " smooth-sliding Mincius," *L.* 86, he intends possibly to convey a suggestion of the passing wind or the river itself playing upon the reeds. It may be also that he calls the reeds " vocal " as being potential pipes. Probably he had something of both conceptions in his mind. Cf. *P. R.* 2. 26, " Where winds with reeds and oziers whispering play." See also Lucretius, *De Rerum Nat.* 5. 1383 ff., and Jerram's note on *L.* 86.

discriminately changed about.   Our modern music lovers might well derive a lesson from the poet in this matter. To most listeners, nowadays, quality of sound seems a matter of small consequence.   There are many compositions which one may seldom hear in their proper setting. Orchestral works become familiar through pianoforte arrangements ; compositions for the violoncello lose their quality when transposed for the violin ; songs are instrumentalized, or set in half a dozen different keys adapted to every pitch and quality of voice.   Few of us seem to have retained that instinctive feeling for the permanence of quality, so characteristic of the older musicians, and of such discerning music-lovers as John Milton.   To him no variation in function was possible without an accompanying variation of quality.   If an instrument can produce different qualities of tone, as is the case with the pipe family, then it can likewise exercise different functions. If its quality and effect are constant, then its function must also be constant.   The instruments already discussed furnish good examples of Milton's consistency of treatment. The organ, because of its imitative characteristics, stands in a class by itself, possessing such a variety of qualities as to render it fit for almost any use—expressive of almost any emotion.   Yet Milton seems to prefer those registers which are peculiar to the organ, such as the diapasons, and to emphasize the loftiness of their sounds.   The instruments of the pipe family, as a rule, give forth tones of a gentle, sad, almost mournful quality.   " Flutes and soft recorders " are especially effective in taming wild passions and producing calmness and nobility of mood.[1]   But under certain conditions the flute or pipe may inspire riotous merriment.   This, however, occurs only amid rustic surroundings, and is not to be considered its natural mood. [2]   Milton's flutes

[1] *P. L.* 1. 551.   [2] *C.* 173.

were not played in the manner of the modern transverse instrument. His conception is always that of the classic αὐλός, a pipe played through a reed mouthpiece, and resembling in shape and style of execution the modern clarinet.

Other instruments whose quality of sound is soft and soothing are the lute and viol, " more apt for mournful things." [1]

The sounds of the lyre and harp possess a lofty grandeur, befitting the characters and emotions of gods and angels.[2]

The trumpet stands for a loud and pervading quality of sound, uttering little music, but useful as a signal, a noise of triumph, of acclamation or of warning. Its brazen quality is expressed in such phrases as " the sounding alchymy,"[3] " sonorous metal, blowing martial sounds." [4] A particularly shrill type of the trumpet tone is produced by " clarions."[5]

The drum is also used at times as a mere signal.[6] But instruments of percussion in general bear for Milton a connotation of horror. There is a hint, too, of the barbaric in their use. The sacrifices of Moloch are accompanied with the "noise of drums and timbrels." [7] His priests and those of Osiris perform their dread rites with " cymbals' ring "[8] and "timbreled anthems dark." [9] The captive

---

[1] *P.* 28.

[2] Among other conventional instruments of Heaven Milton mentions the dulcimer, *P. L.* 7. 596. The source of the allusion is evidently Daniel 3. 5 ; 10 ; 15. The dulcimer of Milton's time was a stringed instrument, played with little hammers. See the description given by Pepys, *Diary,* May 13, 1662. But Milton evidently has in mind the Hebrew dulcimer, which was a wind-instrument similar to the bag-pipe. Certainly this definition gives a better meaning to the passage cited above. See G.

[3] *P. L.* 2. 517.   [4] *P. L.* 1. 540.

[5] *P. L.* 1. 532 ; 7. 443. Cf. the classic *buccina, E.* 4. 117-118.

[6] *P. W.* 2. 45.   [7] *P. L.* 1. 394.   [8] *H.* 208.   [9] *H.* 219.

Samson is led in triumph before his barbaric conquerors to the sound of " pipes and timbrels." [1] Of instruments of percussion Milton also mentions cymbals and bells. For cymbals he implies nothing but contempt. They are mere noisemakers. In *Tetrachordon* he says : " If we understand not this, we are but cracked cymbals, we do but tinkle, we know nothing, we do nothing." [2]

Bells have no specific musical value in Milton, yet he evidently delights in their sound. He echoes the rhythmic rise and fall of their measured tones when he says :

> Oft, on a plat of rising ground,
> I hear the far-off curfew sound,
> Over some wide-watered shore,
> Swinging slow with sullen roar. [3]

Contrast with this description the lines of *L'Allegro* beginning :

> When the merry bells ring round. [4]

There is here more suggestion of actual music. The poet evidently has in mind the chime of bells in a country church.

The word " chime " represents with Milton the most musical of bell-like sounds. As a rule it cannot be accurately defined as anything more than mere harmony or concord, yet at times there seems to be a suggestion of actual vibrating metal in his conception. Thus the celestial spheres are bidden to " ring out,"

---

[1] *S. A.* 1616-1617. See Kircher, *Mus. Univ.* 2. 4. 2, for a description of the Hebrew instruments of percussion.

[2] *P. W.* 3. 366, an obvious echo of I. Corinthians 13. 1. Cf. the contemptuous reference to " those cymbal doctors," in *Eikonoklastes, P. W.* 1. 376.

[3] *Il P.* 73-76.

[4] *L'A.* 93 ff.

> And let your silver chime
> Move in melodious time.[1]

When one compares the " sphery chime " of *C*. 1021, and
the " sphere-metal " of *U. C*. 2. 5, one is tempted to believe that Milton conceived of the spheres as composed
of some metallic substance, whose vibration gave forth
sound.[2]

In *P. R*. 2. 363, Milton contrasts " chiming strings "
with " charming pipes," thus observing the difference
between striking the metal wire and breathing through
a hollow tube.[3] The rustic music of the " loose, un-
lettered hinds " [4] is represented by the rebeck, a primitive style of fiddle,[5] and by the bag-pipe, doubtless intended as a caricature of the sylvan pipe of the real
pastoral.[6] Milton has no great liking for such primitive
popular music. Yet he is thoroughly aware of its characteristics, and, even in his amused contempt, is never
guilty of misrepresenting it. A rebeck or a bag-pipe
would be entirely out of place in the hands of a serious
bard, or among the harmonies of heaven, but as accompaniment to the " riot and ill-managed merriment " [7] of
the rustic dance they possess a distinct musical value.

This appreciation of values, then, is the most significant feature of Milton's treatment of instrumental
music. He seems to recognize instinctively the character
of the instruments to which he alludes, and he evidently
considers this musical character as important as is personality in human beings.

---

[1] *H*. 128-129.

[2] Cf. Pliny, *Hist. Nat*. 2. 3.

[3] Cf. the " silver-sounding instruments " of Spenser's *F. Q*. 2. 12.
71, by which the entire description in *P. R*. is evidently influenced.

[4] *C*. 174.   [5] *P. W*. 2. 73 ; *L'A*. 94. See G.

[6] *P. W*. 2. 73.   [7] *C*. 172.

Of the forms of instrumental music mentioned by Milton little need be said. There were few titles in his time possessing any very definite meaning, as, for example, the symphony or sonata of to-day. When the instrumental music was anything more than mere accompaniment to the voice (in which case it naturally took its name from the vocal form), it was most often in some variation of the dance. Milton is very fond of the figure of the dance, and almost all his instrumental music which does not accompany the voice is dance-music. But his conception of the dance is very different from that of the present day. It is based upon classic foundations, for Greek music included not only the harmony of tones, but poetry and the dance as well. All three possessed the common quality of rhythm, which, for Milton, is of the utmost importance. When he describes the angels of Heaven who

> in celestial measures moved,
> Circling the throne and singing, while the hand
> Sung with the voice,[1]

he presents this triple combination complete.

The rhythm of such a dance must be wholly sublime, without hint of anything light or trivial. Milton's conception of the dance is really threefold. In its best and highest form it is the embodiment of grace and dignity, of pure motion in its most sublime aspect, a mystic expression of the rhythm of nature, as shown in the stars, the seasons, the months and years. In its lower forms, among human beings and the lesser deities, it still retains grace and beauty, but its spirit is purely one of joy, without dignity or sublimity. Finally, when induced by intemperance and base passions, it loses even its grace and beauty, and becomes a mere

---

[1] *P. R.* 1. 170 ff.

wanton expression of sensuality.[1] Milton takes a personal interest only in the first and highest form of the dance. The second he regards with a kind of indulgent amusement, admitting its place in everyday life, but not considering it seriously as a part of music in general. With the third he has no sympathy whatever, but treats it with lofty scorn. Milton's notion of the dance, therefore, is essentially Greek. For him the sublimity of music as a whole compels a belief in the sublimity of the dance as a particular phase of the art. The majesty of rhythm is summed up in it, for it makes visible the motions which underlie all music. It is in itself practically a visible harmony.[2] No realms were too sublime for this perfection of art. He conceived of the planets as moving " In mystic dance, not without song." [3] The motions of the constellations, computing " days, months, and years " are likened to a " starry dance." [4] The whole universe is composed of " terrestial Heaven, danced round by other Heavens." [5] The morning-star " comes dancing from the east." [6] On another occasion Milton asks,

> What if the sun
> Be centre to the world, and other stars,
> By his attractive virtue and their own
> Incited, dance about him various rounds ? [7]

[1] For the classic source of these ideas see Plato, *Laws* 2. 655 ; 656, and Appendix V, pp. 141-142.

[2] " Poetry, music, and dancing constitute in Aristotle a group by themselves, their common element being imitation by means of rhythm—rhythm which admits of being applied to words, sounds, and the movements of the body. The history of these arts bears out the views we find expressed in Greek writers upon the theory of music ; it is a witness to the primitive unity of music and poetry, and to the close alliance of the two with dancing." Butcher, *Aristotle's Theory of Poetry and Art,* 4th ed. p. 139. Cf. *Poet.* 1. 5 ; Plato, *Laws* 2. 655 D.

[3] *P. L.* 5. 178.   [4] *P. L.* 3. 580-581.   [5] *P. L.* 9. 103.
[6] *M. M.* 2.   [7] *P. L.* 8. 122-125.

The dance of the angels is described as

> Mystical dance, which yonder starry sphere
> Of planets and of fixed in all her wheels
> Resembles nearest; mazes intricate,
> Eccentric, intervolved, yet regular
> Then most when most irregular they seem.[1]

Comus speaks of

> the starry quire,
> Who, in their nightly watchful spheres,
> Lead in swift round the months and years.[2]

Milton took this conception of the dance of the stars directly from Plato, *Timaeus* 40 : " Vain would be the labor of telling about all the figures of them moving as in a dance, and their meetings with one another, and the return of their orbits on themselves, and their approximations, and to say which of them in their conjunctions meet and which of them are in opposition, and how they get behind and before one another, and at what times they are severally eclipsed to our sight and again reappear." [3]

The angels express their adoration of the Lord by sublime dances, accompanied by songs and instrumental music.[4] In the creation of Nature the " stately trees " are described, rising " as in dance." [5] In another description,

> Spring and Autumn here
> Danced hand in hand.[6]

---

[1] *P. L.* 5. 620-624.
[2] *C.* 112-114. Cf. also the dance of the Pleiades, *P. L.* **7.** 374.
[3] Jowett's tr. 2. 533.
[4] *P. L.* 5. 161-163 ; 619-620 ; 630 ; 657 ; *P. R.* 1. 170 ff.
[5] *P. L.* 7. 324.
[6] *P. L.* 5. 394-395.

Sometimes this sublimity of motion is debased to wrong uses, as when the priests of Moloch dance " about the furnace blue," or the "night-hag," "lured with the smell of infant blood," goes to " dance with Lapland witches." [1] Yet even in these horrible forms the dance seems to have a certain fascination for the poet.

It is different with the simple dance of pure joy. Here the emphasis is entirely on grace, daintiness, and delicacy. It exhibits little of the "poetry of motion," but much childish delight in movement. Thus the fairies dance.[2] Thus

> universal Pan,
> Knit with the Graces and the Hours in dance,
> Led on the eternal Spring.[3]

Thus the nymphs and the wood-gods constantly disport themselves,[4] and thus poor mortals also at times give vent to their merriment.[5] The distinction between this style of dance and the higher, nobler form is made strikingly clear in Satan's sarcastic comment on the angels struck by cannon-shot, who

> into strange vagaries fell,
> As they would dance ; yet for a dance they seemed
> Somewhat extravagant and wild.[6]

Their motions, in other words, were fantastic enough to suit the popular conception of a dance, yet were unrhythmic and irregular.

[1] *P. L.* 2. 664-665 ; *H.* 210.

[2] *P. L.* 1. 786-787 ; *V. Ex.* 59-64 ; *C.* 118.

[3] *P. L.* 4. 266 ff. ; and cf. *P. L.* 6. 3 ; *P. R.* 1. 57 ; *S.* 1. 4 ; *T.* 2.

[4] *C.* 883-884 ; *A.* 96-99 ; *L.* 34-35 ; *E.* 5. 119 ff. ; *Epit. Dam.* 85 ; *Ad Patrem* 115 ; *Ad Rousium* 8.

[5] *E.* 6. 39 ff. ; *L'A.* 33 ; 95-96 ; *C.* 952.

[6] *P. L.* 6. 614-616.

Finally there is the repulsive and sensual type of dance, for which Milton feels a whole-souled contempt. It is merely erotic, intemperate, characteristic of " luxury and riot," wantonness, " midnight shout and revelry." [1] Bacchic dances, however, as being more poetic in association, and approved by classic tradition, are treated with respect.[2] Milton also applies the figure of dancing to the effervescence of wine or of a drug, possibly with a thought of the resulting intoxication.[3]

It becomes clear, then, that to Milton the dance is not trivial. It is the embodiment of rhythm itself, and therefore of the utmost importance in musical science. So reverent is his attitude towards the classic dance that the abuse of it calls forth from him expressions of bitter scorn.

Of more particular forms of instrumental music Milton has little to say. He refers at times to distinct styles of the dance, such as the jig and the morrice,[4] but without especial interest. He is naturally most familiar with the various forms of organ composition, particularly the fugue, which he describes in a masterly and convincing style.[5] Milton's allusion to the fugue is no mere figure of speech, but denotes a definite style of composition. The fugue of the sixteenth and seventeenth centuries was really a movement in canon form. Morley's definition shows this. He says : " We call that a Fuge, when one part beginneth and the other singeth the same, for some number of notes (which the first did sing)."[6] There were at that time two kinds of fugue—limited fugue, which was in strict canon, and unlimited fugue, which

---

[1] *P. L.* 4. 768 ; 11. 584 ; 714-715 ; *C.* 103-104 ; 143-144 ; 176-177.

[2] *E.* 6. 15 ; *Epit. Dam.* 219.

[3] *S. A.* 543 ; *C.* 673.

[4] *C.* 115-116 ; 952 ; *P. W.* 1. 323 ; 3. 152 ; 158.

[5] *P. L.* 11. 563 ; *P. W.* 3. 476.   [6] Morley, p. 84.

began in canon, but soon broke off into free passages. The latter form, as developed by Frescobaldi,[1] was probably in Milton's mind. Fugue, as we now know it, did not exist until the eighteenth century. When he speaks of "the masterful running over many chords and divisions,"[2] he probably has in mind some fixed style of composition for organ or virginal. Milton evidently had a taste for musical embellishment in its proper place. A bewildering series of passages pleased him because of the mathematical order which lay at the bottom of their confusion, and because of the demands made by it upon the analytic powers of the listener. The involved structure of the fugue-form must therefore have appealed to him very strongly.

Such general types of instrumental music as the " little consorts " and " fantasies " of his own day are almost entirely neglected by Milton.[3] The reason for this is easily found. Aside from its function of accompaniment to the dance, instrumental music has its chief significance for him in its relation to the human voice. Taken by itself it is incomplete and unsatisfactory. But as supplying rhythm, melody, and harmony for the voice, it fulfils its highest function and gives a working foundation for all practical music. Nearly all of Milton's instrumental music directly implies, or at least suggests that it may be the accompaniment of song. And his direct references to song so far outnumber those dealing with instrumental music, and are of so much more personal a character, that no doubt can remain as to the real preference of the poet. To him music is, primarily, song.[4]

---

[1] Cf. note 2, p. 22 above.   [2] *P. W.* 3. 62.

[3] Except in very general or figurative application ; cf. *Il P.* 144-145 ; *H.* 132 ; and possibly *S. M.* 27 ; *P. L.* 5. 296.

[4] He is emphatic in representing Orpheus as exercising his power " carmine, non cithara," *Ad Patrem* 52-55.

Milton's preference for vocal music was a natural one. It must be remembered that he was primarily a poet, and secondarily a musician. To him all poetry in its essence was song, and therefore he felt the strongest appeal in that kind of music which could be combined with verse. Moreover, Milton lived at a time when poetry and music were very closely allied.[1] That his own skill lay chiefly in vocal music is also significant. Finally, the influence of the classical writers must be taken into consideration, for with them the terms " poetry " and " song " were practically synonymous.

That Milton knew something of vocal culture is assured by the statements of Aubrey that he " had good skill," and that he " taught his nephews to sing."[2] But it must be remembered that vocal culture in Milton's day, was very primitive. The placing of the voice, the proper control of the breath and many other demands of modern skill received little or no attention. If a singer could read music at sight and keep a correct pitch, his training was considered adequate, and quality and power were a secondary matter. So Milton's " good skill " must not be rated too highly in the light of modern training. We may assume, however, that a man of Milton's aesthetic sensibilities and painstaking habits would be satisfied with nothing less than the best quality of amateur art. Of his interest in the human voice and his conception of the science of tone production many hints are given all through his works. His English poems alone contain eighty-three references to the voice, many of which have a distinctly musical significance.[3] It is difficult, however, to make a definite analysis of Milton's conception of vocal music. His poetizing tendency continually gets the better

[1] Cf. Chap. I, pp. 8, 11.   [2] *Brief Lives* 2. 64 ; 67.

[3] Cf. particularly *P. L.* 5. 204 ; 9. 530 ; *P. R.* 4. 256 ; *A.* 77 ; *L'A.* 142 ; *S.* 20. 11 ; *H.* 96 ; *C.* 247. See G.

of his scientific knowledge. As a result, confusion frequently arises from his use of technical details to express mystical ideas. In general he may be said to refer all song to a form of motion, the breath causing a vibration of the vocal chords, transmitted, in turn, to the external air. In its details, however, such a technical explanation is, to him, utterly prosaic. Some reason must also be found for the existence of this mysterious force in the human body. It is most simply and poetically supplied by the introduction of a divine agency.[1] To Leonora, singing at Rome, he says " either God, or at least some high intelligence of the deserted heaven, warbles active in secret through thy throat." [2] Practically the same idea is expressed by Comus when he says of the Lady's singing,

> Can any mortal mixture of earth's mould
> Breathe such divine enchanting ravishment ?
> Sure something holy lodges in that breast,
> And with these raptures moves the vocal air
> To testify his hidden residence.[3]

Such a mystical conception as this shows clearly that Milton's chief interest in song is not a technical one. In making this statement the accuracy of his knowledge is not for a moment questioned ; he was undoubtedly well versed in the technique of vocal music, and the various styles of song current in his own day were also familiar to him. His taste seems to lean toward the sacred rather than the secular forms, and references to hymns, anthems, chants, psalms, and other forms of the church service are

---

[1] This is a Platonic conception. See *Phaedrus* 245 ; 265.

[2] *Ad Leonoram* 1. 5-6. Masson's tr., *Life* 1. 804.

[3] *C*. 244-248. Cf. also the influence of Apollo as pictured in *E*. 6. 45-46 ; *Ad Patrem* 66. For classic sources of the conception cf. Claudian, *In Eutropium* 1. 327 ; 2. 46.

frequent.[1]   On the secular side he makes intelligent allusions to such popular contemporary forms as airs, madrigals, ballads, and rounds.[2]

But Milton's conception of vocal music is too broad to
be limited by the set forms of his own day.   His ideals are
far beyond the bounds of technical details.   His spirit is
the classic spirit, and his attitude is that of the Greek.
The single term " music," in the Greek sense, included
the kindred arts of tone, of poetry, and of the dance.
This easily explains Milton's persistent connection of the
three.   But to the Greek mind " poetry " was essentially
" song," and Milton likewise uses the terms almost
synonymously.   He is particularly fond of describing
himself as a singer and his writings as song.   It is thus
that he speaks of his greatest works, *Paradise Lost* and
Paradise Regained :

> I, who erewhile the happy garden sung,
> By one man's disobedience lost, now sing
> Recovered Paradise to all mankind.[3]

Again and again he refers to his other poems in the same
terms.[4]   The great *Nativity Hymn,* when nearing its
close, becomes a " tedious song," [5] and later, in writing
of the Passion, the poet says, " now to sorrow must I tune
my song."[6]   Other poets, prophets, and even speakers
are described at times as expressing their thoughts in
" song." [7]   In the Latin poems of Milton the word *carmen*

[1] Cf. particularly *P. L.* 2. 242 ; 5. 656 ; *P. R.* 4. 335 ; 594 ; *Il P.*
163 ; *H.* 17 ; 219 ; *S. M.* 15 ; *P. W.* 1. 466 ; 2. 61 ; 426. See G.

[2] Cf. *C.* 495 ; *P. W.* 2. 73 ; *S.* 13, *title* ; *P. R.* 2. 362 ; *L'A.* 136 ;
P. 27 ; *C.* 144 ; *P. W.* 2. 57. See G.

[3] *P. R.* 1. 1-3.

[4] Cf. particularly *P. L.* 1. 13 ; 3. 18 ; 413 ; 7. 24 ; 30 ; *P. R.*
1. 12 ; *L.* 186.

[5] *H.* 239.   [6] *P.* 8.

[7] Cf. *P. L.* 7. 107 ; 8. 243-244 ; 9. 25 ; 10. 862 ; *P. R.* 3. 178 ;
L'A. 17 ; *H.* 5 ; *S.* 13. 13 ; *V. Ex.* 45.

invariably has the meaning " verse " or " poetry."[1]
Moreover, in this strictly classic sense, he never represents
the singer as voicing any but his own thoughts. This
conception is most clearly brought out by Milton in his
lines to his father, in which he vigorously defends his own
desire to write *carmina*—in other words, to be a poet.

Milton's first and highest definition of song, then, might
be worded as " The expression of thought in rhythmical
form." It will be noted that in this definition rhythm,
not melody, is the essential quality.

Melody, however, has its place in song, and this appears
in a more concrete meaning, also modelled on classic lines,
which Milton often employs. According to this more
definite conception, song is the chanting of words to instrumental accompaniment. In such song there is little
melody in our modern sense, yet the conception is distinctly different from that of his fundamental definition,
" all poetry is song." It is in this more concrete fashion
that Milton most frequently describes song. All his most
idealized types of singing, the bards of ancient and medieval times, Apollo and the Muses, Orpheus, the greatest
lyric poets, and particularly the celestial choirs are represented thus.[2] It will be noticed that the identity of
singer and composer is still insisted upon. The angels of
Heaven instinctively sing in harmony, for, even though
each individual may be improvising, the subject is the
same for all—the praise of the Creator. Even the fallen
angels produce ravishing music, their celestial instinct
still remaining with them, although their song now is but
" partial," that is, a matter of individual taste, having
lost its spirit of community.[3] It is this sublime chanting

[1] Cf. *E*. 5. 5; 6. 5; 6; 14; *Ad Patrem* 17; 21; 24; 26; 33; 37; 41; 53; 55.

[2] *Cf.* especially *P. L.* 3. 372 ; 383 ; 6. 886 ; 7. 182 ; 5. 161 ; 1. 6 ;
Il P. 48 ; 105 ; *V. Ex.* 37, and Glossary, s. v. *song*.

[3] *P. L.* 2. 552 ff. See Appendix I, p. 114, note 1.

to instrumental accompaniment which is really Milton's ideal of song. If the motions of the dance are added, the Greek idea is complete, and the whole of musical art is realized. When Milton speaks of poetry as song, he really identifies the poet with the ancient bard, and his expression must therefore be taken not as mere metaphor, but as uttering a very concrete and definite conception. The classic influences are thus even more evident in Milton's conception of vocal than in that of instrumental music. He is forced, nevertheless, to recognize also the merits of the contemporary style of song.

This leads him to a third conception, the most concrete, the most technical, the least poetic of all. According to the music of his own time, song is merely melody set to words. Rhythm is a secondary matter. Harmonic combinations and the variations of pitch are all-important. The verse is of no consequence whatever. In fact, the words of such a popular form as the madrigal may be wholly meaningless—mere doggerel. It follows that the composer of the music is clearly differentiated from the composer of the words. The lyric poet, in the classic sense, no longer exists. Any one can improvise a melody or parts, provided that the words be already set. In such a style of song there is slight appeal to Milton, the poet.[1] He is forced to admire the skill exhibited in part-singing.[2] He is fascinated by the perfection of technique implied by the " wanton heed and giddy cunning " of the " melting voice through mazes running."[3]

[1] Cf. *S.* 13. 1-4.

[2] He probably possessed considerable ability himself. See *Earliest Life*, p. 21 : " He had an excellent ear, and could bear a part both in Vocal and Instrumental music."

[3] *L'A.* 141-142. These words illustrate again Milton's love of an " orderly confusion " already brought out in the description of the organist, *P. L.* 11. 561 ff., and of the dance of the spheres, *P. L.* 5. 620 ff.

But even such complicated measures fall far short of the sublimity of real poetry. His sonnet to Harry Lawes shows clearly his contempt for the ordinary song-writers of his day. They insult the verses which are intrusted to them. They " scan with Midas' ears." To Lawes alone can he say with truth,

> Thou honour'st Verse, and Verse must send her wing
> To honour thee, the priest of Phoebus' quire.[1]

Except in such particular instances, song, as mere melody set to words, can assume no real importance in Milton's mind.[2]   He is glad to put it into the mouths of the cheerful peasants.[3]   It fits well enough the " serenate which the starv'd lover sings."[4]   In fact, for the average mortal this style of song is quite satisfactory. But mere imitative skill can never hope to compete with the creative instinct which is characteristic of song in the best sense of the word.[5]

Milton may be said to think of song in still another way when he applies the term to mere sound without words. Strictly speaking, however, this is but a symbolic representation of the melodic style of song just described, and his usage may be considered as simply metaphorical. Such are his frequent allusions to the song of birds.[6]   Yet these allusions are not merely conventional. The birdsong is represented as possessing a very definite quality, a characteristic emotional effect, as is the case with musical instruments. This is especially true of Milton's

---

[1] *S.* 13. 4 ; 9-10. Cf. Appendix II.

[2] Milton was evidently so much impressed with the ability of Lawes that he even allowed him to make alterations in the text of *Comus.* See Appendix II, p. 125, note.

[3] *L'A.* 65.   [4] *P. L.* 4. 769. Cf. *P. L.* 11. 580-584.

[5] Cf. above, p. 52.

[6] *P. L.* 3. 39 ; 4. 603 ; 5. 7 ; 41 ; 198 ; 7. 433 ; 8. 519; *L'A.* 7 ; *Il P.* 56.

favorite, the nightingale, who is described as singing " her amorous descant " in harmony with all Nature.[1]   So also the bee sings " at her flowery work." [2]   Instrumental accompaniment to vocal music is poetically expressed by the phrase " the hand sung with the voice." [3]   Similarly, in giving the call to arms, " the matin trumpet sung."[4] Such metaphors as these, however, scarcely require a separate classification.

Milton's conception of vocal music may therefore be summed up as threefold.   Essentially, all poetry, every rhythmical expression of thought, is song.   As such it is the highest form of art.   More concretely considered, such song is represented by the chanting of words to instrumental accompaniment, which, indeed, is the actual form in which the ancient bards uttered their poetry. Lastly, song must be considered in its technical contemporary sense, as melody fitted to words, or even melody without words, in which case the term " song " may be applied metaphorically to the sounds of birds and even of musical instruments.

In Milton's conception and use of the art of music, then, the most significant point is his tendency to poetize the actual, concrete elements and materials of the art. He takes the common facts of instrumental and vocal music as he finds them, and then exalts them to the level of his own poetic imagination.   To him, musical instruments are not mere structures of wood, strings, and brass. They are organisms inspired with life of a universal reality, dead things " pierced " with the " inbreath'd sense " of the " sphere-born harmonious sisters, Voice and Verse." [5]

---

[1] *P. L.* 4. 603.   See the discussion of descant below, Appendix I, p. 116.

[2] *Il P.* 143.   [3] *P. R.* 1. 172.   [4] *P. L.* 6. 526.

[5] *S. M.* 2-4.

They perform definite functions and possess definite characters. They are the concrete representatives of basic musical reality. Just as the laws of mathematics must be learned if one would be in touch with the absolute entities, so the technique of instrument or voice must be mastered in order that one may grasp the sublime truths of music. And there can be no doubt as to the thoroughness of Milton's technique. He knows the instruments in all their details. He knows the mechanism of the human voice as well as it could be known in his day. But he is not satisfied with the mere conception of a vibrating set of vocal chords. He demands a soul, a divine power, to set the mechanism in motion, to cause it to utter not mere unintelligible noise, but immortal verse.[1] What mathematician, what physicist would stop at the mere learning of set formulas which any one can commit to memory? Of what use would his knowledge be to him, if it did not bring him closer to ultimate reality? Similarly, says Milton, why should a musician be satisfied with the technical formulas relating to instrument and voice when they stand ready to lead him on through the laws of Nature itself to some ultimate truth?

Thus interpreted, Milton's knowledge of the art of music becomes something infinitely greater and more significant than that of even the skilled composers of his day. It is a knowledge whose details fit into his whole philosophy of life, a knowledge which assures him of the bond of union between the aesthetic and the ethical, a knowledge which leads him to a conviction of reality and of the final purposes of God Himself.

[1] For the Platonic origin of this conception, see Appendix V, p. 139.

IV

MILTON AND THE THEORY OF MUSIC

Milton was no mere dabbler in music—no dilettante, seeking amusement and culture with the smallest possible expenditure of effort. He took all his interests seriously, believing that what was at all worthy of attention was worthy of thorough and detailed study. His attitude towards music was primarily that of a painstaking scholar. Yet Milton's scholarship was of a kind which necessarily tends towards mysticism. Music had for him a much deeper significance than that of a mere accidental, interesting phenomenon, or even of a highly developed art. A hint as to the nature of this deeper significance has already been given in the preceding chapter. A consideration of his theory of music leads one even further in the same direction, and results in a revelation of the entire mystical philosophy of the poet. Biographers are here of little assistance, and our conclusions must be drawn mainly from his works. Judged by these Milton's theory of music may be said to consist of two kinds, which may be termed roughly the scientific and the metaphysical. By the first is meant that part of musical theory which is based upon mathematical truths, and is therefore assumed to possess objective reality. The second includes the conceptions of the origin and nature of music, and of its mystic relationship to the whole universe. Both phases of Milton's theory were derived by him from classical sources, both were developed by him in the light of contemporary scholarship, and both received the stamp of his own individuality in the final form which they took in his mind.

Strictly speaking, the Greek theories of music can scarcely be called scientific. Plato had expanded the mystical Pythagorean system of numbers, without making its mysticism more intelligible. Aristotle had criticized without illuminating. Aristoxenus, Plutarch and Claudius Ptolemaeus had made successive attempts at interpretation without carrying conviction to their readers. Finally, Boethius had collected all the material and pretended to expound it, the result being, in the main, a meaningless jumble of vague definitions. It is not necessary for us here to attempt an analysis of this complex mass of ancient theory. Our study is concerned only with its effect upon Milton, and it is sufficient for us to know that he found a definite meaning in much that to us is unintelligible, that he was able to discern unerringly which ideas had a permanent value, and that he succeeded in adapting this material to the conditions of thought in his own time.

Milton's natural love of the orderly and the mathematical inspired in him a more than usual interest in the so-called " measurable music." The Pythagorean system of numbers, the necessary relationships of concord and discord, the mysteries of " proportions " in pitch and rhythm, exercised upon him a peculiar fascination which is reflected in numerous allusions throughout his works. He regards number and measure as essential in music, because they give it objective reality and permanence. Without this mathematical foundation, music, as a science or even as a scientific art, could not exist. And since number and measure are universal, music is therefore an essential and inherent part of the universe.[1]

---

[1] Cf. Plato, *Timaeus* 69, " When all things were in disorder, God created in each thing, both in reference to itself and other things, certain harmonies in such degree and manner as they are capable of having proportion and harmony." — Jowett's tr. 2. p. 560.   For

Poetry is so closely connected with music that their fundamental laws are in large part the same. Therefore poetry also may be said to gain universality not only through its idealistic handling of truth, but through its dependance on number and measure as well. With such a conception as this, it is only natural that the poet should emphasize the scientific or mathematical element in music. He speaks of the

> secret power
> Of harmony, in tones and numbers hit
> By voice or hand, and various-measured verse.[1]

He describes the planets which

> move
> Their starry dance in numbers that compute
> Days, months, and years.[2]

The heavenly music is composed of

> the innumerable sound
> Of hymns and sacred songs.[3]

An elaborate play on scientific musical terms is contained in the *Lines on the University Carrier* :

> Time numbers motion, yet (without a crime
> 'Gainst old truth) motion numbered out his time.[4]

a detailed explanation of the Pythagorean system of numbers, see Boeckh, *Kleinere Schriften* 3. 169 ff. Cf. also Jowett's tr. of Plato, 2. 455 ; 490. Plutarch devotes four chapters to an exposition of the theories of Plato and Aristotle (Westphal's ed. *De Musica* 16-19, tr. pp. 49-51). See also Boethius, Paul's tr. 38-60, and Plato's *Republic* 7. 522-532.

[1] *P. R.* 4. 254-256.   [2] *P. L.* 3. 579-581.   [3] *P. L.* 3. 147-148.
[4] *U. C.* 2. 7-8. Cf. also *P. L.* 3. 37 ; 345 ; 5. 150 ; 8. 19 ; 113 ; 10. 888 ; *Ad Patrem* 51 ; 58 ; *Ad Rousium* 48 ; *P. W.* 3. 117.

" Motion " (besides its general philosophical sense) seems to bear in Milton a twofold musical significance. Its more general meaning is that of actual motion productive of sound, as the vibration of a string or of the air, or the whirling of the spheres. Thus the " silver chime " of the " crystal spheres " is said to " move in melodious time,"[1] and in *Comus* the song of the lady is described as due to " something holy " which " moves the vocal air." [2]   But " motion " may also refer to the variations of musical numbers, the change of pitch, or the modulations of harmony.[3]   Thus Milton speaks of " thoughts that voluntary move harmonious numbers " [4] and the lines

> My heart, which by a secret harmony
> Still moves with thine,[5]

have almost certainly at least a secondary musical significance. [6]

Milton's conception of " motion " is thus necessarily complex. He is attracted by the various possibilities of the idea, and he uses it in that all-inclusive fashion which is so characteristic of his treatment of expressions pregnant with meaning. In other words, his conception of motion is limited neither to the actual nor the theoretical. It is a combination of both in all their possible phases. To him all music is motion, and all motion is potentially music. Music not only begins in actual motion, but continues in motion and can manifest itself only in motion. A single note, continuing unchanged, would still imply some actual motion as its cause, and as soon as another

---

[1] *H.* 128.

[2] *C.* 247. Cf. also *P. L.* 3. 580 ; 5. 177 ; 618 ; *C.* 116 ; *L.* 180.

[3] See the discussion of the subject in Morley, p. 202 ; Macran's translation of Aristoxenus, pp. 170-171 ; Boethius 1. 3 ; and below, Appendix V, pp. 137-139.

[4] *P. L.* 3. 37.   [5] *P. L.* 10. 358-359.   [6] Cf. also *U. C.* 2. 7.

note is added, giving the basis of melody or harmony,
there is not only the fresh motion of new vibrations, but
the progression through the interval from one note to the
other as well.[1]

The word " measure " was very generally applied to
music in Milton's own time and in a variety of meanings.[2]
Its commonest significance pertained to rhythm, and any
form of rhythmical dance was loosely called " a measure."
It is in this sense that Milton uses the word in *Comus*,
when he introduces a heading, " The measure," in the
manner of a stage-direction. But Milton's general conception of " measure " is much broader than the mere
idea of a dance. To him all real music was measurable,
and the word could therefore express either rhythm or
correctness of intervals—in fact, anything directly connected with the mathematical proportions of music.
In the *Arcades* he describes music as that which can

> keep unsteady Nature to her law,
> And the low world in measured motion draw
> After the heavenly tune.[3]

Milton is particularly fond of the word " proportion "
as applied to music.[4] It was a term still common in the
music of his own time, and was applied to relations both

[1] Cf. the definition of " motion " in Grove's *Dict.*

[2] The expression " measurable music " represented an idea,
based upon the Pythagorean theory, that correct music could be
composed through a mere knowledge of the mechanical laws govern-
ing the art. As a result much music was composed which was
entirely unmelodic and valuable only as an exercise. It was an
idea analogous to the prevalent modern theory that technical
correctness is sufficient to create art, whether it be in music,
painting, or literature.

[3] *A.* 70-72. Cf. also *P. L.* 9. 846 ; *P. R.* 1. 170 ; *S.* 2. 10 ; *P. W.*
2. 418 ; 3. 135.

[4] See Glossary.

of pitch and of rhythm. Interesting discussions of the subject may be found in Morley and Boethius,[1] and Milton probably depended on both of these, as well as on some of the older authorities, for his knowledge. The poet believed that all harmony and all rhythm were due to certain distinct mathematical proportions, and that these existed throughout the universe in the same manner as in music.[2] Owing to this very general application, it is not always possible to read musical significance into Milton's use of " proportion." In a few cases, however, his meaning is unmistakeable. A good example is the visionary organist whose improvisations lead him " instinct, through all proportions low and high." [3] The importance of " proportion " in the universe is shown in the lines *At a Solemn Music*, when

> disproportioned Sin
> Jarred against Nature's chime, and with harsh din
> Broke the fair music that all creatures made.[4]

The captive Samson bewails the lack of harmony in his nature. His bodily strength is " immeasurable," his wisdom " nothing more than mean." " These two, proportioned ill, " drove him " transverse." [5]

In his conceptions of harmony, of concord, and of discord, Milton shows closest dependence upon classic sources. In fact it is difficult to understand his notion of harmony unless one refers to his Greek originals. His use of the terms " symphony " and " harmony " often gives the impression that they are synonymous. This,

---

[1] See Morley, pp. 31, 241 ; Boethius 1. 7 ; 16-19 ; 2. 8-31 ; 3 (entire) ; 4. 1-13 ; and Appendix V, pp. 138-139.

[2] Cf. *C.* 773 ; *P. L.* 5. 479.   [3] *P. L.* 11. 562.   [4] *S. M.* 19-21.

[5] *S. A.* 209. See Appendix I, p. 123. Cf. also *P. L.* 8. 385 ; 9. 711 ; 936 ; *C.* 330 ; *P. W.* 1. 233 ; 2. 90.

however, is a false interpretation of their meaning. The distinction between the two terms is made clear by a comparison with the Greek ἁρμονία and συμφωνία. In the classic usage, " harmony " has the general meaning of an adjustment or fitting together of parts. It is used particularly as denoting a scale or a system, whose parts have been adjusted in their proper relations. With the modern sense of harmony, as distinguished from melody, it has, of course, nothing in common. Milton uses the term in a larger sense to include everything within the sphere of music showing definite system or relationship. The word " symphony," however, in the Greek sense, can be applied only to the sound of two tones in concord. It is confined within very definite limits. To the Greeks only three intervals constituted concords—the fourth, the fifth, and the octave, known respectively as διατεσσάρων. διαπέντε, and διαπάσων.[1] Any one of these combinations might thus be termed a " symphony." The meaning of the term could therefore be included in that of " harmony," but could not possibly be identical with it. It is impossible to say how strictly Milton adhered to the rigid principles of concord and discord laid down by the Greeks. Of the various kinds of " symphony " mentioned above he names only one, the octave or *diapason*. He applies this term most fittingly, as the " perfect concord," to the harmony which existed between Heaven and Earth before " disproportioned Sin " had jarred the music of the universe.[2] Aside from this one instance we find no mention of any actual Greek συμφωνία. He speaks much of concords and discords, of

[1] The sum of two or more octaves, the sum of one or more octaves and a fourth, and the sum of one or more octaves and a fifth would also be counted as concords, because of the perfect concord of the octave. See Aristoxenus 20.

[2] *S. M.* 19-24.

consonance and dissonance in general, but gives no hint of the musical intervals which he may have had in mind.[1] The distinction between harmony and symphony is made particularly clear in two passages in which both terms are used together. The first refers to

> the sound
> Symphonious of ten thousand harps, that tuned
> Angelic harmonies.[2]

The meaning here is obvious. The " angelic harmonies " are merely the general system of celestial music. In order to take part in it, the sound of the harps must be " symphonious," that is, in perfect concord. The second passage occurs in the description of the celestial music in the *Nativity Hymn*, when the spheres are commanded to " ring out " in honor of the Savior's birth,

> And with your nine-fold harmony
> Make up full consort to the angelic symphony.[3]

In other words, the system of the sphere-music, when added to the concord of the angels, gives the effect of a complete orchestra.[4]

---

[1] Cf. *P. L.* 2. 497 ; 967 ; 3. 371 ; 6. 210 ; 311 ; 897 ; 7. 32 ; 217 ; 9. 1124 ; 10. 707 ; 12. 29 ; *S. A.* 662 ; 1008 ; *S. M.* 17 ; 26 ; *C.* 550 ; *P. W.* 1. 161 ; 176 ; 241 ; 3. 237.

[2] *P. L.* 7. 558-560.   [3] *H.* 131-132.

[4] The word " symphony " is sometimes used by Milton as meaning a band or choir, and may possibly have that significance here. Cf. *P. W.* 2. 479, " harping symphonies," and *P. W.* 3. 476, " the whole symphony." In the mere sense of " concord," cf. *P. L.* 1. 712 ; 3. 368 ; 5. 162 ; 11. 595 ; *P. W.* 1. 232. The line " loud symphony of silver trumpets blow " appears in the second draft of the *Solemn Music* 11. Milton may have discarded it partly because the use of " symphony " would be technically inaccurate as applied to trumpets, which, in Greek music, never played any concord except unison.

Milton's uses of the more general term " harmony " are many and various. At times he seems almost to personify " harmony," as when

> in their motions Harmony divine
> So smoothes her charming tones that God's own ear
> Listens delighted,[1]

or when he speaks of

> Untwisting all the chains that tie
> The hidden soul of harmony.[2]

There is in the poet's conception a " secret power of harmony." [3] It controls the laws of Nature and the universe. It alone can " hold all Heaven and Earth in happier union."[4] Such harmony as this is much more than mere musical concord. It is system, adjustment, relationship, proportion, considered as fundamental law.[5]

Milton's Hellenized conception of the theory of music becomes still more noticeable in his treatment of such details as the construction and relation of scales, and of the various keys or " modes." Greek music recognized three *genera* of melody—the diatonic, the chromatic, and the enharmonic.[6] Of these the first was by far the most useful and, in fact, the only one which maintained a permanent value. Curiously enough, the only one of the

---

[1] *P. L.* 5. 625-627.

[2] *L'A.* 143-144. Cf. his personification of Discord, *P. L.* 2. 967 ; 10. 707 ; *In Quint. Nov.* 142, and see Plutarch, *De Musica*, Westphal's tr., p. 54, in which the comic poet Pherecrates is quoted as representing Harmony as a female figure abused by Timotheus of Miletus, and bound by him with twelve strings.

[3] *P. R.* 4. 254-5.   [4] *H.* 108.

[5] Cf. also *P. L.* 2. 552 ; 3. 38 ; 4. 687 ; 10. 358 ; *P. R.* 2. 362 ; *A.* 63 ; *S. M.* 2 ; *P. W.* 1. 232 ; 279 ; 2. 80 ; 90 ; 408 ; 3. 217 ; 346 ; 476 ; and see Glossary.

[6] Cf. Macran's *Aristoxenus* 1. 19.

classes specifically named by Milton is the *chromatic*.
The reference occurs in a variant reading in the second
draft of the *Solemn Music*, where the poet speaks of

> leaving out those harsh chromatic jars
> Of clamorous sin that all our music mars.[1]

The distinctive feature of the chromatic *genus* was its
use of quarter tones.   The resulting harmonies may well
have " jarred " upon the simple combinations of the
diatonic scale.[2]

Even though he may seem to neglect the *genera*, Milton
shows a thorough understanding of the ancient "modes"
or keys of the diatonic scale.   Only three are of importance—the Dorian, the Phrygian, and the Lydian, corresponding roughly to our modern keys of E minor, D minor,
and C minor, respectively.[3]   Of these Milton obviously
prefers the Dorian, and in this he adheres closely to the
sentiments of Plato.[4]   Plato will admit only the Dorian
and Phrygian modes into the music of his Republic.   He
describes the Dorian mode as one " which will sound the
word or note which a brave man utters in the hour of
danger and stern resolve, or when his cause is failing, and
he is going to wounds or death, or is overtaken by some
other evil, and at every such crisis meets fortune with
calmness and endurance." [5]   Milton, in his account of the
march of the fallen angels, gives a description of the effects
of the Dorian mode which echoes in a remarkable fashion
this passage from Plato.

---

[1] *Cambridge Facsimile*, p. 5.

[2] Cf. also *S. A.* 662 ; *S. M.* 20 ; *P. L.* 2. 880 ; 6. 315.

[3] See Glossary.

[4] Cf. Elbert N. S. Thompson, *Controversy between the Puritans
and the Stage*, pp. 11 ; 18 ; 24.

[5] *Rep.* 3. 399, tr. Jowett, 2. 222. Cf. *Laches* 188.

Anon they move
In perfect phalanx to the Dorian mood
Of flutes and soft recorders—such as raised
To highth of noblest temper heroes old
Arming to battle, and instead of rage
Deliberate valour breathed, firm and unmoved
With dread of death to flight or foul retreat ;
Nor wanting power to mitigate and swage,
With solemn touches, troubled thoughts, and chase
Anguish and doubt and fear and sorrow and pain
From mortal or immortal minds.[1]

Such a description as this shows clearly that it was not so much the structure of the ancient modes that appealed to Milton, but rather the ἦθος or characteristic emotional values represented by them. The significance of the Dorian mode is frequently emphasized by him. Possibly he has in mind its primitive severity when he calls the song of the shepherd lamenting the death of Lycidas a " Doric lay." [2] It certainly enters into his description of " Aeolian charms and Dorian lyric odes," [3] and into the satirical passage in the *Areopagitica* in which he says that "no song must be set or sung but what is grave and Doric." [4] Milton's own verses are praised by Sir Henry Wotton as possessing a certain " Doric delicacy." [5]

Milton only once refers to the Lydian mode, for its ἦθος evidently does not please him. Plato describes it as " a soft or drinking harmony," not fit for men of character,[6] and it is significant that Milton's single reference occurs in the description of purely sensuous music.[7]

---

[1] *P. L.* 1. 549-559.

[2] *L.* 189. The chief reason for using the term is, of course, the fact that Theocritus wrote in the Doric dialect.

[3] *P. R.* 4. 257.   [4] *P. W.* 2. 73.

[5] See the letter prefixed to *Comus*.

[6] *Rep.* 3. 399, tr. Jowett, 2. 222.   Cf. *Laches* 188.

[7] *L'A.* 135-150.

Aside from such specific allusions, there is a suggestion of the ἦθος of the Greek modes in such lines as these, from the *Passion* :

> For now to sorrow must I tune my song,
> And set my harp to notes of saddest woe,

and

> Me softer airs befit, and softer strings
> Of lute, or viol still, more apt for mournful things.[1]

To Milton, then, the important feature of the Greek modes was not their pitch, nor their succession of intervals, but their effect upon man, their power to induce joy or sadness, heroic valor or effeminate languor. It is the natural attitude of the poet towards music, accepting without question that which appeals to the ingeniousness of man, but dwelling with particular pleasure upon that which appeals to the emotions.

But Milton's poetizing tendency goes far beyond the scientific details of music. It makes of his theory of music a mysticism which is far more important than his technical knowledge, for here he gives his imagination the greatest freedom, and impresses his own individuality most distinctly upon the materials which are at his command. One might almost say with truth that Milton's entire theory of music is mystical. He recognizes the scientific aspect of music, it is true, and he rejoices in the reality of music which is implied in its highly mathematical nature. But the ultimate reality of it for him lies far beyond the world of science and the reach of human understanding. This mysticism is with Milton by no means a conventional matter derived from pagan mytho-

---

[1] *P.* 8-9 ; 27-28. Cf. also *L.* 87 ; *S. A.* 662 ; and see below p. 86.

logy, but in its essence a sincere belief, amounting to religious faith. From Greek philosophy and mythology he has gained the conception of a divine origin of music, of a harmony arising from creation itself, of a system of concords connecting Heaven, Earth, and the Spheres, and running through all Nature. In the Scriptures he finds hints of a musical Heaven, of choirs of angels, singing to the accompaniment of the harp. He retains the elements of both conceptions and combines them into a system of his own, in which the universal harmony has as its object the praise of the Creator, and in which the spheres join in some mysterious fashion with Christian spirits and angels to produce a complete concord, inaudible to man until he shall succeed in escaping from the bonds of sin. Such a theory as this of Milton's is rather poetical than purely philosophical. His purpose is frankly not that of critical, scientific inquiry, but of developing to their fullest extent the poetical possibilities of his material. His conception transcends the laws and limitations known to man. It is metaphysical.

Milton's conception of the universe as musical presents at times an aspect distinctly pagan; at other times it seems completely Christian. The mysticism common to both is the bond between the two phases.

One of Milton's first public exercises at Cambridge was on the subject of the music of the spheres, showing how early he had laid hold upon a definite conception which appeared again and again in his later poetry.[1] In this youthful essay the poet argued that Pythagoras did not intend his "music of the spheres" to be taken literally, but only as representing the necessary harmony in the relations

---

[1] *De Sphaerarum Concentu.* See Appendix IV and Masson, *Life* 1. 279.

of the celestial orbs and their obedience to fixed law. It was only through the misrepresentations of Aristotle that the idea of an actual musical harmony arose. After all, why should not space be filled with actual music? Ancient mythology shows that such a belief was universal. The stories of Arion, of Apollo, of the Muses dancing day and night, from the first beginning of things, around Jove's altars, all point in the same direction. And what if no one now living has ever heard this starry symphony? May it not be merely because our own ears are not able or worthy to hear the sounds? If we, like Pythagoras, "bore pure, chaste, snow-clean hearts," then we should undoubtedly apprehend this sweetest music, and all things should " return immediately as if to that golden age."

Even in this youthful exposition Milton dwells upon the ethical significance of the sphere-music. The scientific foundation of the theory troubled him little. From his classical sources he received various explanations. In Plato's *Republic* [1] he read of that strange journey of Er to the other world, where the structure of the universe was revealed to him, with the motions of the eight planets in their spheres, and the spindle turning on the knees of Necessity. This account told him also of the Sirens sitting on the upper surfaces of the circles, each one " hymning a single sound and note." Thus a ἁρμονία was formed. Cicero's *Somnium Scipionis* gave him a more detailed and less allegorical explanation. According to it, the sounds were caused by the " impulse and motion of the spheres themselves," it being " impossible that such prodigious movements should pass in silence." Moreover, these sounds were so powerful that human hearing could not comprehend them, " just as

---

[1] *Rep.* 10. 617, tr. Jowett, 2. 449.

you cannot look directly upon the sun, because your sight and sense are overcome by his beams."[1]

In addition to these classical sources, Milton must have been familiar with the interpretation given by Boethius,[2] and with the elaborate diagrams of a universal music in the works of Robert Flud and of Morley.[3] He found various references to the sphere-music in Chaucer, Shakespeare, Spenser, and Sylvester's *Du Bartas*.[4] Being influenced by all these Milton's own conception is necessarily somewhat indistinct and not always consistent. It is important to note, however, that he interprets the Greek ἁρμονία in its technical meaning of a system or a scale.[5] Just as the human soul, according to Plato, is a " harmony," so also the universe in general is a system controlled by definite laws. Such being the case, the question of the actual sounds of the spheres, their causes and their effects, is really of minor importance. Milton, with a poet's privilege, deliberately disregards the possible arguments concerning these minor points, and insists upon the universality and the ethical significance of the system. He accepts the allegory of the Sirens, as is shown by the lines *At a Solemn Music* and by the fine passage in the *Arcades* which really sums up his conception.[6] But he finds the physical reason for the music in the motions of the spheres themselves.[7] Moreover he

---

[1] *Somnium Scipionis*, tr. Edmonds, p. 295. Cf. Macrobius, 2. 1-4 ; Pliny, *Hist. Nat.* 2. 3 ; and see below, Appendix V, pp. 144-146.

[2] Paul's ed. 1. 27. Cf. Nichomachus, ed. Meibom, lib. 2, p. 33.

[3] Flud's diagram is given in Hawkins 4. 169 ff. Cf. Morley, p. 228, and see below. App. V, p. 149.

[4] *Parliament of Fouls* 60 ff. ; *Merchant of Venice* V. sc. i ; *Hymn to Beauty* 197-200 ; *Du Bartas* 2. 2. 4. 718-727.

[5] See above, p. 63.

[6] *S. M.* 2 ; *A.* 63 ff. See Appendix V, p. 144.

[7] Cf. *P. L.* 3. 482 ; 580 ; 5. 177 ; 7. 500 ; 8. 19 ; 125.

gives to the earth a species of motion which must certainly be productive of sound.[1]   This earthly music was
once " in tune with Heaven " and formed a part of the
great system or harmony, but sin caused a discord, after
which all Nature was disturbed and it became impossible for man to hear the heavenly music.[2]   This
consists not only of the universal sphere-harmony, but
of the actual songs and instrumental symphonies of
the celestial beings as well.   In order to have any part
in this universal music man must purify his heart and
become sinless once more, in other words, recover that
innocence the loss of which created the disturbance
described in *P. L.* 10. 650 ff.   The decidedly Christian
aspect thus given to the pagan myth is the mark of
Milton's own individuality.[3]   He finds a conception of
universal harmony, allegorically stated, possibly resting
on a scientific foundation.   For some reason the music
is inaudible to human ears.   Various explanations are
suggested, most of them hinting vaguely at the grossness
of mankind, unable to appreciate divine things.   Milton
however, makes the conception very definite.   Before sin
entered into the world, he says, man *was* able to hear the
heavenly music.[4]   Even now a man may hope to attain
to some degree of apperception and appreciation by ridd-
ing himself of the fetters of sin.   And when he once
leaves this world and joins the heavenly choirs, he
becomes again a part of the universal music and finds
therein complete harmony.   The passages in which Milton

[1] Cf. *P. L.* 8. 130 ; *A.* 71.   [2] Cf. *P. L.* 10. 650 ff.

[3] He was probably influenced in this by the Neo-Platonism of
Plotinus, and of the Italians, Ficino, Pico della Mirandola, and
others.   See the general discussion of the subject in Harrison's
Platonism in English Poetry 167-221.

[4] In his essay, *De Sphaerarum Concentu*, he speaks of this golden
age as occurring before Prometheus stole the divine fire.   See
Appendix IV, p. 135, l. 12.

illustrates this conception are numerous. At times the scientific facts of contemporary astronomy conflict with his theory. He is forced to admit that the sun, not the earth, is the centre of our universe.[1] But this does not affect the music of the spheres, which is caused, as in the Greek conception, by the motions themselves. The origin of these motions is explained by the fact that

> the great First Mover's hand
> First wheeled their course.[2]

The figure of a dance is a popular one with Milton to describe such motions.[3] The inaudibility of the sphere-music is reasserted in various ways. Besides the passage in the *Arcades*, which speaks of the

> heavenly tune, which none can hear
> Of human mould with gross unpurgèd ear,[4]

we have an interesting account in the *Nativity Hymn* in which the spheres are called upon to " bless our human ears," if they " have power to touch our senses so." [5] The *Apology for Smectymnuus* contains a reference to the " celestial songs to others inapprehensible." [6] The Elder Brother's Platonic description of the soul in *Comus* refers to the heavenly " things that no gross ear can hear " —undoubtedly a suggestion of the sphere-music.[7]

That the inability of man to hear the celestial music is due to the intervention of sin is shown most clearly in the lines *At a Solemn Music* 17—18. The Heaven there

---

[1] Cf. *P. L.* 3. 581 ; 8. 122 ff.   [2] *P. L.* 7. 500-501.

[3] Cf. *P. L.* 5. 177-178 ; 7. 374 ; 9. 103. See also above, pp. 43-45.

[4] *A.* 72-73.   [5] *H.* 126-127.

[6] *P. W.* 3. 122. Cf. Rev. 14. 3.

[7] *C.* 458. Cf. also *C.* 997 ; *P. L.* 3. 193 ; 8. 49.

described is not the *Coelum stellatum* of the sphere-myth, but a Christianized Heaven as the dwelling-place of God. The use of the word " diapason " would seem to indicate that the sound of the earthly music is exactly an octave below that of Heaven.[1] If this is the case, a systematic scale of tones represented by the spheres can not be consistently applied.[2] To Milton, however, the important point here is not so much the completeness of the system as the perfect concord of the octave. The manner in which the earthly music corresponded to that of Heaven is well illustrated by the morning song of Adam and Eve, in innocence, who lacked neither " various style," nor "holy rapture,"

                              to praise
    Their Maker, in fit strains pronounced, or sung
    Unmeditated ; such prompt eloquence
    Flowed from their lips, in prose or numerous verse,
    More tuneable than needed lute or harp
    To add more sweetness.[3]

This pure music of the golden age was sung by a universal choir at the birth of the Savior :

    Such music (as 'tis said)
    Before was never made,
    But when of old the Sons of Morning sung,
    While the Creator great
    His constellations set,
    And the well-balanced world on hinges hung.[4]

It is possible, however, that this earth may once again be made worthy of hearing the heavenly music.

---

[1] Cf. *S. M.* 23 ; *A.* 70-72.

[2] Cf. Kircher, *Mus. Univ.* 10. 2, in which such a scheme is attempted.

[3] *P. L.* 5. 147-152.

[4] *H.* 117-122.   Cf. the account of the of the music of " the Sons of Morning," *P. L.* 7. 253 ff. ; 275 ; 594 ff.

> For, if such holy song
> Enwrap our fancy long,
> Time will run back and fetch the Age of Gold.[1]

At the close of the *Comus* a hint is given that, by means of Virtue, the sphere-music may become audible to human ears.

> She can teach ye how to climb
> Higher than the sphery chime ;
> Or, if Virtue feeble were,
> Heaven itself would stoop to her.[2]

When Milton describes the music of the angel choirs his conception loses all its vagueness and becomes decidedly concrete. Christianity supplies him not with abstractions, but with most realistic images. There is an actual music of Heaven in which voices and instruments alike join. It is accompanied by the sounds of the universe, resulting in one great orchestral harmony in praise of the Creator.[3] On the day of rest,

> not in silence holy kept : the harp
> Had work and rested not ; the solemn pipe
> And dulcimer, all organs of sweet stop,
> All sounds on fret by string or golden wire,
> Tempered soft tunings, intermixed with voice
> Choral or unison.[4]

The celestial music is variously described as

> the innumerable sound
> Of hymns and sacred songs,[5]

---

[1] *H.* 133-135.   [2] *C.* 1020-1023. Cf. *U. C.* 2. 5.
[3] See Appendix V, p. 149.
[4] *P. L.* 7. 594-599. Cf. the purely pagan Heaven of the *Epitaphium Damonis* 215-219, and that of the corresponding part of *Lycidas*, 179-180.
[5] *P. L.* 3. 147-148.

and as

> Loud as from numbers without number, sweet
> As from blest voices, uttering joy.[1]

The emphasis placed on the lack of " number " or system suggests that the heavenly music is unrestrained by any of the limitations known to man—which would explain also Milton's indifference to a systematic arrangement of the sounds of the spheres, such as that given by Plato and others.

But the most vivid description of the celestial music occurs in the *Nativity Hymn*. Here the theme is first announced by the angel choirs:

> Divinely-warbled voice
> Answering the stringed noise,
> As all their souls in blissful rapture took :
> The air, such pleasure loth to lose,
> With thousand echoes still prolongs each heavenly close.[2]

Nature recognizes the import of the music.

> She knew such harmony alone
> Could hold all Heaven and Earth in happier union.[3]

Finally the entire universe is compelled to join in the music :

> Ring out, ye crystal spheres!
> Once bless our human ears,
> If ye have power to touch our senses so;
> And let your silver chime
> Move in melodious time,
> And let the bass of Heaven's deep organ blow ;
> And with your ninefold harmony
> Make up full consort to the angelic symphony.[4]

[1] *P. L.* 3. 346-347.   [2] *H.* 96-100.   [3] *H.* 107-108.
[4] *H.* 125-132. For other references to the celestial music see below, App. I.

Milton's universal harmony is otherwise manifested than by the spheres and the heavenly choirs. All Nature is full of sounds which combine naturally to produce music.[1]   As the descriptions of this earthly music of Nature occur chiefly in the *Paradise Lost*, when sin had as yet caused no jarring discord, it may be assumed to be a part of the universal harmony. It has the same characteristics as the heavenly music—instinctively concordant, yet untrammeled by the fetters of proportion or numbers. This is made clear by the description:

> Nature here
> Wantoned as in her prime, and played at will
> Her virgin fancies, pouring forth more sweet,
> Wild above rule or art, enormous bliss.[2]

The conception cannot be other than musical, and the " fancies " may well be taken technically in the sense of the instrumental " fantasies " (or " fancies ") of Milton's own time, as well as in its general meaning.

The completeness of the universal harmony is nowhere made more clear than in the majestic lines which represent the orisons of Adam and Eve. All the parts of the universe are there called upon in turn to glorify the Creator. First of all the angels, who

> with songs
> And choral symphonies, day without night,
> Circle his throne rejoicing.[3]

Next come the Sun and Moon, and then the

> five other wandering Fires, that move
> In mystic dance, not without song.[4]

---

[1] See Appendix V, pp. 148-149, for possible sources of Milton's descriptions.

[2] *P. L.* 5. 294-297.   [3] *P. L.* 5. 161-163.   [4] *P. L.* 5. 177-178.

The music descends gradually towards the earth.

> Air, and ye Elements, the eldest birth
> Of Nature's womb, that in quaternion run
> Perpetual circle, multiform, and mix
> And nourish all things, let your ceaseless change
> Vary to our great Maker still new praise.[1]

Finally, after the " mists and exhalations," the clouds and the showers have been summoned, the various voices of Nature on earth are called to join in the music :

> His praise, ye Winds, that from four quarters blow,
> Breathe soft or loud ; and wave your tops, ye Pines,
> With every plant, in sign of worship wave.
> Fountains, and ye that warble, as ye flow,
> Melodious murmurs, warbling tune his praise.
> Join voices, all ye living Souls ; ye Birds,
> That singing up to Heaven-gate ascend,
> Bear on your wings and in your notes his praise.
> Ye that in waters glide, and ye that walk
> The earth, and stately tread, or lowly creep,
> Witness if I be silent, morn or even,
> To hill or valley, fountain, or fresh shade,
> Made vocal by my song, and taught his praise.[2]

To Milton every thing in Nature is capable of sound.

> Airs, vernal airs,
> Breathing the smell of field and grove, attune
> The trembling leaves.[3]

Brooks " warble " as they flow.[4]   Streams " murmur ".[5] The sounds and seas " in wavering morrice move." [6]

---

[1] *P. L.* 5. 180-184.

[2] *P. L.* 5. 192-204.   A similar sense of the music in Nature is reflected by Spenser in *F. Q.* 2. 12. 33 ; 70-71 ; Tasso, *G. L.* 15. 55. 56 ; 16. 12.

[3] *P. L.* 4. 264-266.

[4] *P. L.* 3. 31.   [5] *P. L.* 4. 260 ; 453 ; 7. 68 ; 8. 263.   [6] *C.* 116.

The trees arise " as in dance ".[1]   At the first discord of
sin, " Nature, . . . sighing through all her works gave signs
of woe, that all was lost ".[2]

The song of the birds is naturally a part of the music
of Nature.

> Sweet is the breath of Morn, her rising sweet,
> With charm of earliest birds.[3]

> From branch to branch the smaller birds with song
> Solaced the woods, and spread their painted wings,
> Till even ; nor then the solemn nightingale
> Ceased warbling, but all night tuned her soft lays.[4]

There is a reality in all this natural harmony.   It is
not merely figurative.   To the blind Milton, at the time
of writing the largest part of *Paradise Lost*, all external
appearances are blotted out.   Sounds only remain.   The
only harmony which he can possibly find in his universe
is a musical harmony.   If it seems imperfect at present,
the time will surely come when it will be perfected.

This mystical faith is the foundation of Milton's entire
theory of music.   Without it his system would possess
little more than a technical interest.   Regarded simply
as a musician, Milton might well be commended for his
scientific accuracy in details and for his thorough knowledge of the fundamental laws of musical theory.   At the
same time he would necessarily be severely criticized for
attempting to extend the bounds of scientific music, for
making free use of his imagination where actual experience
failed him. As a poet, however, Milton carries conviction by
those very qualities which, from the standpoint of the mu-

---

[1] *P. L.* 7. 324.

[2] *P. L.* 9. 783-784.   Cf. *P. L.* 9. 1001-1003 ; 2. 714 ff.

[3] *P. L.* 4. 641-642.

[4] *P. L.* 7. 433-436.   Cf. also *P. L.* 2. 494 ; 4. 603 ; 771 ; 5. 6 ff.;
16 : 40 ; 394-395 ; 7. 443 ; 9. 198-199 ; 800 ; 846.

sician, would be considered a superfluity or even a handicap.
It is a proof of his greatness that no sharp line of division
can be drawn between his ideas of music and of poetry,
just as it is the proof of the greatness of a philosopher
that no barrier need separate his ideas of science from
those of his religion. A noble, Christian soul, imbued
with the spirit of poetry, cannot possibly isolate one of
the fine arts from his inner life, and make it the object
of mere reflective consciousness. He must either overlook
it entirely, or make it a definite part of his own existence.
Thus Milton's theory of music is really only a part in his
theory of the universe. His experience teaches him that
the laws of harmony are in some mysterious way the
expressions of ultimate reality. If only they are carried
far enough they will be found to possess universal validity.
His philosophical instincts once satisfied, Milton proceeds
as a Christian, throwing over his whole conception the
poetic glamor which the Scriptural allegories themselves
justify. With God as the central controlling source,
the infallibility of his system need not be questioned.
It is above and beyond all laws known to man. God has
created the universe in a secret harmony of which we
have but an inkling in the laws of mathematics and of
music—a harmony which pervades not only the heavens
and the celestial choirs, but the planets in their spheres,
the elements, and even all Nature and the creatures of
earth. Such is the mystic sublimity of the conception
to which Milton is brought by his theory of music.

V

THE SIGNIFICANCE OF MILTON'S KNOWLEDGE OF MUSIC

A mere record of facts, statistics, and observations regarding Milton's knowledge of music is of little value except as it adds to our knowledge of the mental and spiritual life of the poet. How slight, after all, is our acquaintance with the inner workings of a soul such as that which we call Milton! How futile would be any attempts to systematize accurately his manner of thought! Our information concerning him is necessarily limited to two sources—his biographers, whose testimony is not always unimpeachable, and his own writings, which are too often open to a variety of interpretations. Whatever is not directly and definitely imparted to us from these sources must be sought out by laborious analysis and painstaking comparisons. In this study of Milton's knowledge of music, therefore, the final aim must be not to draw up a table of statistics, but to show how these accumulated details may increase our knowledge of the spirit of the man Milton.

The first question to be considered is that of the relation of Milton to his time. How, as illustrated by his interest in music, did Milton's mind compare with the minds of his contemporaries? It would be a mistake not to regard him as the natural product of his time. He was not an exception, a unique prodigy, living apart from his environment, and having no share in its intellectual life. The influences which affected him were the same as those which affected other poets and other musicians. The difference between Milton and his contemporaries lay not in the materials which presented

themselves to him, but in the way in which these materials
were utilized—in other words, in his mental habits themselves.   Milton differed from most other men of his
generation in that he was a thinking man.   The Cavalier
was not conspicuously intellectual.   And, though the
Puritans really claimed the right of private judgment,
yet even the most independent of them were so possessed
of a single idea that their thought was stunted into bigotry.
But Milton thought always.   The breadth and depth of
his mind are nowhere better shown than in his treatment
of music.   The materials at his command were here the
same as those used by any other musician of his time ;
but how completely they were transformed by his powers
of thought !   The dependence on the classical writers
on theory, for instance, was common to most scholarly
musicians of the seventeenth century.   Even though
little understood, the Greek music was still considered
the basis of all systems of harmony.   But, while to its
originators the Greek theory really meant something, its
principles had become, to the minds of the seventeenth
century, mere lifeless formulas.   Milton approached
Greek music in a different spirit.   To him, as a lover
of the classics as well as of music, these ancient theories
had reality and life.   They were parts of a great philosophy, a great system of thought.   They showed how
the experience of the universe affected their originators.
This universe was still the same ; his own experience was
similar to theirs ; the laws laid down in ancient times had
proved constant.   What wonder, then, that Milton should
have appropriated and expressed the Greek theory in
all its pristine purity ?   To him human thought was one
continuous process, dealing with one continuous problem.
Even nowadays we are too much inclined to conceive of a
distinct break somewhere between the past and the present.   We are apt to think of ancient art, ancient music,

ancient literature as incompatible with our own civilization. To Milton there was no such break. He identified himself with antiquity as truly and as completely as with his own time. His debt to the classics is therefore wellnigh immeasurable. From them he derives his philosophical attitude towards music, his respect for its laws, his reverence for its mystical attributes. What in an ordinary mind would import a mere scholarly interest is with Milton a deep feeling, a firmly-grounded faith, inherent in his spiritual life.

But he owes much also to contemporary music and musicians, both English and Italian. From the latter, in particular, he learns the practical possibilities of the art. He studies the best compositions, hears the best performers on various instruments, himself acquires the ability to express his own thoughts through the medium of voice or instrument. He sees the real manifested in the empirical. By direct contact with music as thus revealed to him, his poetical imagination is inspired. The individuality of an instrument becomes to his fancy an actual personality. The human voice becomes a manifestation of divine spirit. But it is on its technical side that contemporary music influences Milton most decidedly. The most striking point concerning his references to music, and one which has always been noted by commentators, is his unfailing technical accuracy. Whether it be a matter of the art or the theory of music, whether it has to do with voice or instrument, performance or composition, Milton's allusion is always technically and minutely correct. As a result, his musical metaphors possess a strength and a consistency which the casual reader often fails to appreciate. This technical accuracy Milton owes to his very thorough knowledge of contemporary music, acquired not only through the teaching of his father, but through constant practice and intercourse with skilled musicians as well.

The important influence thus exerted by the art of music throughout his life resulted in an idealization of harmony in his mind. The prevalence throughout the universe of an actual musical harmony constantly suggested to him the possibility of a general, spiritual harmony within himself and among men. It was an ideal never realized by the poet on earth, for his own life was one peculiarly lacking in harmony. In his university days he was secluded and often discontented, misunderstood by his fellows, possibly also misjudged by his masters. Later he fell out with the church and fought to unseat the bishops. His domestic troubles were notorious. His divorce pamphlets involved him in public controversies. He was continually buffeted by jarring political factions. He strove to defend free speech against Presbyterian oppression, and again to vindicate the cause of English freedom in the face of all Europe. His theology was a subject of dispute with others and even within himself. After losing his eyesight in the service of his country he was doomed to endure the downfall of his cause, and in the triumph of his enemies barely escaped with his life. In spite of such discords his ideal of harmony remained constant.

What light, then, does Milton's love of music, admitting its importance in his life, throw upon his character as a whole ? It reveals him first as a philosopher, second as a poet, and finally as a Christian. Each of these phases of his character must be considered in turn.

His philosophy, in the first place, enables him to find ultimate reality in music. It induces in him a love of the mathematical, of the scientifically accurate. His knowledge of mathematics and of the mathematical properties of music leads him to suppose that their underlying laws are universally valid. This Platonic idea is the real basis of his conception of music. Such an idea actually implies a metaphysical system and is essentially mystical. In a nature like Milton's, however, the philosophical ideas cannot well be separated from the poetical. The two must be studied together.

Milton's philosophy, even though it may be the foundation of his musical interest, is speedily subordinated to his poetry. His imagination is stronger than his reason. This conquest, however, is by no means involuntary, but quite deliberate. Milton's mind is not incapable of abstract reasoning. He prefers, however, to give free rein to his poetizing tendency. Milton, the poet, is constantly reflected in his treatment of music. On the side of the art of music his poetical nature manifests itself in his attitude towards musical instruments, which he invests with individual personalities and consistency of character. His conception of the voice also is poetical. It is to him the direct manifestation of the human soul, of some divine agency hidden in the body or the mind. Song is essentially the same as poetry. For written poetry is unnatural and a late development of civilization. Primarily, poetry is vocal in character. As poetry is song, and, as song is the expression of the soul and hence of God, the poet really expresses the divine in Nature. On the side of the theory of music, Milton's poetizing tendency is even more marked. He attempts to express with concrete images that abstract universal reality which has been suggested to him by the Greek philosophy of music. He adopts the allegory of the spheres. He gives to each part of Nature its concrete and audible sounds. It is the poetry and the philosophy of such a conception that appeals to him.

The ethical value of music is also of supreme interest to the poet. The Greek notion of the ἦθος of the modes is continually reiterated by him. He is not concerned so much with the abstract qualities of music as with its definite, concrete effect on man, its power to produce joy or sadness, to inspire heroic valor, or to induce effeminate languor. It is true that the ethical in music belongs to philosophy rather than to poetry. In Milton's case, however, the ἦθος appeals more to his imagination than to his reason. As a philosopher he would be concerned primarily with the cause of the ἦθος, and would attempt to formulate its laws in the abstract. As a poet, however, he is interested chiefly in the effect. He accepts the practical manifestations of music as he finds them. From his own actual experience and the records of history and mythology his imagination is supplied with unlimited material.

But there are other and more particular ways in which Milton, the poet, makes use of his knowledge of music. The most noticeable affects his attitude towards language as such. Milton's control of English requires no comment. He plays with words and manipulates them with the dexterity of a linguistic master. His classical training enables him to view a word in all its shades of meaning, its etymological significance, its life as part of a living language.[1] His use of a word often shows that he has several meanings in mind. In some cases he practically descends to deliberate punning. He is fond at all times of metaphorical conceits. These tricks of language are particularly noticeable when Milton is dealing with musical terms. Often he uses a word which has acquired a general meaning, but originally possessed a musical significance. In such cases one can

---

[1] Cf. Hegel's use of such a word as " aufheben," which contains at the same time three separate meanings —to destroy a thing in its original form, to restore it in another form, and to elevate it upon a higher plane.

actually see in his repeated use of the word a shading off, as it were, from the technical to the general meaning. When the direct musical application is impossible, the original significance still seems to haunt him. The psychological effect of such a word on Milton is easily traceable. A good example is the term " noise." In a strictly musical sense it means an instrumental or vocal band, or its music, with the added connotation of a certain amount of complexity. With this definite musical significance Milton uses it when he speaks of the " stringed noise " [1] of the heavenly choirs, and of " that melodious noise " in the *Solemn Music*.[2] The musical connotation is still prominent when he speaks of the nightingale that shuns " the noise of folly," [3] and of the " noise of drums and timbrels."[4] The music implied in the term gradually disappears, but the connotation of complexity develops into that of confusion. This is the significance which Milton is most fond of employing. He speaks of the " noise of riot," [5] " noise, other then the sound of dance or song," [6] " the noise of endless wars," [7] " the noise of conflict," [8] " infernal noise," [9] " a jangling noise of words,"[10] and he puns upon the meaning when, in *Samson Agonistes*, the question, " What noise, mercy of Heaven, what hideous noise was that ? " is answered with the counter-question, " Noise call you it, or universal groan " ?[11] It is not a confusion of sounds, in other words, but has the effect, rather, of a unison. A striking passage, making clear this sense of confusion, is the following :

> At length a universal hubbub wild
> Of stunning sounds and voices all confused,
> Borne through the hollow dark assaults his ear

---

[1] *H.* 97.   [2] *S. M.* 18.   [3] *Il P.* 61.   [4] *P. L.* 1. 394.
[5] *P. L.* 1. 498.   [6] *P. L.* 8. 243.   [7] *P. L.* 2. 896.   [8] *P. L.* 6. 211.
[9] *P. L.* 6. 667.   [10] *P. L.* 12. 55.   [11] *S. A.* 1508-1511.

> With loudest vehemence ; thither he plies
> Undaunted, to meet there whatever power
> Or spirit of the nethermost abyss
> Might in that noise reside.[1]

The term then develops the meaning of mere sound, while the connotation of loudness is a comparatively late addition.[2]

Even more interesting as illustrating such shades of meaning is Milton's use of the word " charm." In a musical sense it means to him merely " song," or as a verb, " to sing," being derived as he believes, directly from Latin *carmen*. Milton's etymology is not correct in this case. Strictly speaking " charm " is not a direct descendant of *carmen* but a dialect variant of " cherme," which is a common 16th century form of " chirm." As such it is used in its primitive sense only in reference to the song of a choir of birds. Milton uses it thus when he speaks of the " charm of earliest birds." [3] Whether correct or not, etymologically, Milton's development of " charm " is extremely interesting. He is the only writer cited in *N.E.D.* to give it the general meaning of " song " or " melody." He uses it thus when he speaks of " Aeolian charms and Dorian lyric odes." [4] But he is unable to rid himself of the connotation of a subduing influence, which already mingles with the primitive meaning in " the bellman's drowsy charm," [5] " charming pipes," [6] and possibly " charming symphonies " [7] also, where instrumental accompaniment is implied.

The natural development of this double significance is towards the idea of a song which has some mysterious

[1] *P. L.* 2. 951-957.   Cf. also *C.* 170 ; *S.* 12. 3.

[2] Cf. *P. L.* 2. 64-65 ; 6. 487 ; 10. 567 ; *C.* 369.   See Glossary and *N. E. D.* s. v. *noise*.

[3] *P. L.* 4. 642 ; 651.   [4] *P. R.* 4. 257.   [5] *Il P.* 83.

[6] *P. R.* 2. 363.   [7] *P. L.* 11. 595 ; 3. 368.

power, a song which casts a spell over the hearer.   In
this sense it may be applied to such phrases as " charmed
their painful steps," [1] " with jocund music charm his
ear," [2] " in Adam's ear so charming left his voice." [3]
The best example is the familiar passage in *Comus*,

> How charming is divine philosophy !
> Not harsh and crabbed, as dull fools suppose,
> But musical as is Apollo's lute. [4]

From this to the general meaning of " magic " is but a
short step.   Thus in the *Comus* we find " charmed cup " [5]
and " the might of hellish charms." [6]   To complete the
evolution, the general meaning of mere " attraction " or
" attractiveness " may be added. [7]

Often a musical metaphor is hidden in a phrase of
seemingly general meaning, and can be detected only
after a close examination.   When, in *Samson Agonistes*,
the " sayings of the wise " seem " harsh and of dissonant
mood from his complaint," the strength of the metaphor
lies in the fancied conflict between two of the ancient
Greek modes—an attempt, as it were, to produce harmony by playing in two widely different and discordant
keys. [8]   When the " blustering winds . . . with hoarse
cadence lull seafaring men o'erwatched," the one musical

---

[1] *P. L.* 1. 561.   [2] *P. L.* 1. 787.

[3] *P. L.* 8. 2. Cf. also the description of Orpheus as Clio's
" enchanting son," *L.* 59.

[4] *C.* 476-478. Cf. also *P. L.* 11. 132 and the use of *carmen* in
Ad Mansum 69.

[5] *C.* 51.

[6] *C.* 613 ; cf. *C.* 150. So also " if there be cure or charm,"
P. L. 2. 460 ; " charm pain for a while," *P. L.* 2. 566.

[7] Cf. *P. L.* 4. 498 ; 9. 999 ; *P. R.* 2. 213. One has only to look
into some of Milton's variant readings to see these psychological
processes actually going on, in other fields as well as in that of music.

[8] *S. A.* 662.

term immediately brings to mind an actual song, in the manner of a lullaby.[1] Such figures as these illustrate Milton's extraordinary sense for sound. He often seems to prefer to describe in terms of sound rather than in terms of form or of color. The mere suggestion of something audible makes his descriptions remarkably vivid. At times this suggestion is practically onomatopoeia, as in such a phrase as the " liquid lapse of murmuring streams." [2] His descriptions of unpleasant sounds are equally effective. The gates of Hell are opened with a " jarring sound, . . . and on their hinges grate harsh thunder." [3] There is onomatopoeia also in such phrases as " sonorous metal blowing martial sounds," [4] and " clashed on their sounding shields the din of war." [5]

Milton's sense for sound is most marked in one of his earliest works, the *Nativity Hymn*. The entire poem seems to move upon an undercurrent of music. It is thoroughly and essentially a song. This is shown at the very start by the appeal to the "Heavenly muse" for some verse, hymn, or "solemn strain." [6] Later it is recalled again and again by the suggestions and direct descriptions of sound. The poem falls naturally into three parts which are distinguished through the characterization of sounds. ⌠The first part is introductory. It is a description of universal peace without a discordant note. It creates a background of complete silence for the great sounds which are to follow at the birth of the Savior. ⌡ This background is made more effective by the negative description of sounds :

---

[1] *P. L.* 2. 286-288.   [2] *P. L.* 8. 263.

[3] *P. L.* 2. 880-882. Cf. the " harmonious sound on golden hinges moving," when " Heaven opened wide her ever-during gates," *P. L.* 7. 205-207.

[4] *P. L.* 1. 540.   [5] *P. L.* 1. 668.   [6] *H.* 17.

> No war, or battle's sound,
> Was heard the world around ;
>
> . . . .
> The trumpet spake not to the armèd throng.

To complete this picture of " peaceful night " there is a suggestion of the gentle sounds of nature in the " whispering " of the winds over the waters, " while birds of calm sit brooding on the charmèd wave."

The second part of the poem consists of a description of the universal harmony at the Savior's birth. It begins with the first soft notes of the angelic song :

> Divinely-warbled voice
> Answering the stringed noise.

The air echoes and re-echoes the sound. Nature awakes to the realization that the harmony has begun which alone can " hold all Heaven and Earth in happier union." Cherubim and Seraphim, " harping in loud and solemn quire," join in the angelic music. Finally even the spheres "ring out " in praise of the Savior's birth, accompanied by the " bass of Heaven's deep organ." The universal music is now complete. Milton seems to feel himself the leader of a tremendous orchestra, which responds to every suggestion of his imagination. If only this universal harmony could continue, then would the age of gold return once more.

> Yet first to those ychained in sleep
> The wakeful trump of doom must thunder through
>   the deep.

There is an abrupt transition from the celestial to the infernal, from the harmonious to the discordant. This transition is again effected by the suggestion of sounds. Thus the third part of the poem is introduced, in which the poet describes the effect of Christ's birth upon various pagan superstitions and the allies of Satan. Their overthrow is portrayed chiefly by the silencing of characteristic sounds connected with their rites. It again illustrates Milton's habitual identification of religion with concord and of irreligion with discord.

> The oracles are dumb ;
> No voice or hideous hum
> Runs through the archèd roof in words deceiving.

Apollo leaves Delphos " with hollow shriek " of despair. In the mountains there is a " voice of weeping " and of " loud lament." The genius of the wood departs "sighing " from " haunted spring and dale." The household gods " moan with midnight plaint."

> A drear and dying sound
> Affrights the flamens at their service quaint.

In vain the priests of Moloch, " with cymbals' ring," call upon the grim idol, " in dismal dance about the furnace blue." In vain the sorcerers of Osiris perform their rites " with timbreled anthems dark." Thus, from beginning to end, the *Nativity Hymn* is built up on suggestions of sound. Its lyric effectiveness lies largely in this preference of the audible to the visible.

In Milton's later works this tendency to describe in terms of sound is still predominant. Possibly it increased with his blindness. It is only natural to suppose that after all images of color and form passed out of his experience, his mind formed its pictures chiefly through the medium of sound. To him the first impression of a forest would be not the green but the whispering of the leaves ; the most vital point in his perception of a stream would be its murmuring sound. The delights of sound are clearly expressed in such a passage as the opening of the Third Book of *Paradise Lost*, in which Milton, bewailing his blindness, calls upon light. He finds consolation only in the music of Nature, the " flowery brooks " which " warbling flow," and the " nocturnal note " of the " wakeful bird." [1]

Milton's sense for sound is rooted in an instinct for harmony. For it is not sound alone which pleases him, but harmonious sound, or at least sound as a part of a potential harmony. Of discord in any form he has a horror. It is to him the direct evidence and manifestation of evil in the universe.

Milton is truly a poet-musician. These two gifts of his nature are mutually helpful. His music is of practical value to his poetry in that it gives him a true sense of rhythm and a fine appreciation of melodious sounds. His poetry reciprocates by idealizing his music so as to raise it above the level of a mere art. To Milton, music is able to express every variety of human emotion. In *L'Allegro* it represents the climax of joy.[2] In *Il Penseroso* on the other hand, the mood of deepest contemplation is consummated in music.[3] The sublimity of music is constantly implied by Milton. Conversely his sublimest passages show a tendency to express themselves in musical terms.[4]

Finally may be cited Milton's use of the conventionalities of musical mythology. Here again his knowledge of music is affected by his poetical instincts. The stories of Apollo and the Muses, of Orpheus and the power of his song, of nymphs and satyrs skilled in music, appeal most potently to his imagination. He delights in the classic formula of calling upon the Muse for aid ; but this conventionality is retained, in the main, rather for his love

---

[1] *P. L.* 3. 30-40.   [2] *L'A.* 135-150.   [3] *Il P.* 161-166.
[4] Cf. *P. W.* 2. 418, quoted p. 111, Appendix I.

of music than for his love of mythology or of the precedent of epic poets. A distinctly musical idea is usually the basis of his thought. In fact, Milton takes occasion to employ the musical attributes of the pagan deities wherever possible, even when such details are not an essential part of the original myth.[1] In his use of the classic pastoral also, Milton shows a tendency to dwell upon the musical elements much more than have other imitators of the form—more indeed than Theocritus and Virgil themselves. Milton's inclination to read a musical significance into everything possible touches even his use of historical material. He reminds us that the ancient Druids were bards and hints at a possible musical worship of Apollo in Britain.[2] This is also reflected in the opening of his *History of Britain*, where the British worship of Apollo is specifically mentioned.[3]

But, curiously enough, Milton finds his most concrete musical images not in paganism, but in Christianity. The music of paganism gives him philosophical abstractions which lead to a vague mysticism. He finds therein hints of a necessary universal concord which appeals to his philosophical nature, but which he is unable to express

[1] Thus he enlarges upon the musical powers of Bacchus, *E.* 6. 14 ; 33-34 ; and of Circe, *C.* 252-256. In *C.* 963-965 ; *P. L.* 11. 132-133, he emphasizes the unusual attribute of Mercury as a musician ; cf. Osgood, *Mythology*, pp. 13, 42.

[2] *Ad Mansum* 35 ; 38-43. Warton notes that Milton here " avails himself of a notion supported by Selden on the *Polyolbion*, that Apollo was worshipped in Britain. See his *Notes on Songs* viii, ix. Selden supposes also that the British Druids invoked Apollo. And see Spanheim on *Callimachus*, vol. ii. 492 ff." Cf. also Milton's constant use of musical figures to describe the works of the ancient poets, *P. R.* 4. 257-260 ; *Ad Mansum* 4 ; 7 ; 9 ; 50-51 ; *Ad Leonoram* 2. 1 ; *In Obit. Praes. Eli.* 18-20 ; *S.* 8. 12 ; *P. W.* 2. 57.

[3] *P. W.* 5. 175.

in philosophical terms. Only in the symbolism of Christianity can he find a definite expression of this mysticism. As a poet he can adopt such allegories as the music of the spheres and of Nature. As a Christian, however, he is able to bring the entire conception to a sublime climax in a Heaven filled with the music of singing angels, and dominating the great harmony of the universe.

Milton is more completely and thoroughly a Christian than either philosopher, poet, or musician. His inner life begins and ends with Christianity, and everything is made to conform to it. There is nothing narrow in Milton's type of Christianity. It is free from Puritan fanaticism. It is so broad as to be potentially all-inclusive. This is made particularly clear by Milton's philosophical adaptation of music to Christianity. How much of this idealization possesses reality for him, and how much is imaginary? What does Milton really mean by " harmony " as constituting the essence of God? Does he believe that an actual system of musical concords runs through all Nature and the universe, including the elements, the planets in their spheres, and the angels of Heaven? Obviously his conception cannot be interpreted thus literally, even allowing for his poetical imagination.[1] A deeper significance must be sought. The real importance of Milton's conception of music lies in the fact that it is a figurative representation of his deepest religious beliefs and aspirations. The cardinal point of Milton's religion is the doctrine of obedience, of conformity to law. It is a rigorist conception, having little in common with the modern notion of the love of God. Milton's God is the Kantian categorical imperative personified. This conception appears again and again in his works. The *Treatise of Christian Doctrine* is full of

[1] Cf. his explanation of the Pythagorean theory, *De Sphaerarum Concentu*, Appendix IV.

allusions to the sin of disobedience.[1]   Milton's greatest
poems, *Paradise Lost, Paradise Regained, Samson Agonistes*, and to a certain extent the *Comus*, are built upon
the theme of obedience.   Paradise is lost through " man's
first disobedience." [2]   It is regained through the obedience of the Savior to his Father's will.[3]   Samson's
tragic guilt lies in his disobedience.[4]   The snares of Comus
are powerless against the Lady's obedience to the laws
of chastity.[5]   The influence which Milton's doctrine of
obedience had over him is shown even in the details of his
domestic and religious life.   To him the position of woman
was properly that of servant and helpmeet to the man.
This belief in its harshest aspect is revealed in his treatment of the character and position of Eve, and in his
divorce pamphlets.   His ideal of religion on earth was
a *church government*, founded upon a definite and revered
law.[6]   The blind devotion to obedience is really the most
Puritanic side of Milton's Christianity.   But it becomes
both softened and elevated when expressed in the poetical
terms of music.   Music, to Milton, represents law and order.

> Such sweet compulsion doth in music lie,
> To lull the daughters of Necessity,
> And keep unsteady Nature to her law,
> And the low world in measured motion draw
> After the heavenly tune.[7]

The systematic adjustment of the entire universe to law
can be due only to the command of a divine Will.   It is
only through obedience to this law that the world can
exist.   Man, by his disobedience, lost his understanding
of the harmony of the universe.   It became inaudible

[1] See particularly the chapter on original sin, *P. W.* 4. 253 ff.
[2] *P. L.* 1. 1.   [3] *P. R.* 1. 1-5.
[4] Cf. particularly *S. A.* 373-380.
[5] Cf. *C.* 766 ; 782 ; 801 ; 418 ff.
[6] Cf. *P. W.* 2. 441 ff.   [7] *A.* 68-72.

to his ear.   But the harmony exists, nevertheless, in spite of man's ignorance thereof.   When he has once freed himself from the bonds of sin, and entered into the celestial life, he will become a part of that harmony and will understand its complete significance.   This musical allegory shows clearly a belief in the immanence of God in Nature and the universe.   It is by no means a pantheism.   But it represents God as the " first Mover," the divine source of all law and order, spreading his influence continually through all that which he has created.   God is to Milton more than an isolated power, setting in motion machinery which thereafter runs mechanically.   He not only starts the machinery, but continues to control it, and makes his influence felt in its every detail.   This is the law, the order, the harmony, of which music represents only a single phase.   Such a conception of religion is far beyond the ordinary Puritanism of Milton's day.

This, then, is the significance of Milton's conception of music.   He has found in it *cosmos*, the " order that shall satisfy one's reasonable soul," amid apparent chaos.[1]   It is a Platonic conception—strictly speaking a Pythagorean conception—yet it bears fruit of a thoroughly Christian character.   It is a conception of supreme importance in ancient philosophy, yet just as vital in modern thought. Is it not true ?   Is not the search for harmony instinctive in mankind now as well as centuries ago ?   Our experience is still the same.   The laws of " measure " in time and space are necessary facts in our lives.   Kant showed that they must be an element in anything of which we are to have any conception whatever.   As long as man exists he will continue to seek to fathom the meaning of those laws which control him so absolutely, of which he feels himself a part, but whose nature still remains a

[1] See Walter Pater's admirable discussion of the " doctrine of number " in his *Plato and Platonism*, pp. 45-52.

mystery. Pythagoras was said to be able to perform miracles. He possessed the key to the riddle of the universe.[1] Through the perfection of his own life he came to an understanding of the cosmic life, of the great harmony of which he was a part. He was, as it were, a musician thoroughly familiar with his instrument. He could play upon it whatever he desired. He could disregard set forms, and improvise according to his own will. He could even change its intervals and tune it according to an entirely new system. But to the uninitiated, the ordinary mortal, dull of ear, clogged up and muddy of soul, this instrument must for ever remain a mystery. He could touch it, procure possibly a faint, mysterious response, but his own will would be powerless to frame laws for it, to impose an arbitrary harmony upon it. He must take conditions as he finds them. To a sincere Christian the Pythagorean fable suggests a striking truth. It is Christ himself who has proved himself worthy to play upon this mysterious instrument of the universe. He is the supreme example of Divinity in man, of the complete and understanding harmony with Nature and God. Christ himself was Milton's ideal. It was the harmonious life—harmonious with man, with Nature and with God—for which he strove.[2] It was this ideal which made him a musician, for in the realm of music he found an actual satisfaction which he could never attain in the world of man. For this reason, also, he delighted in those ancient stories of musicians who, by the power of harmony within them, solved the harmony of the uni-

---

[1] Cf. Milton's description of him, *De Sphaerarum Concentu*, Appendix IV, pp. 134-135.

[2] Cf. *P. W.* 3. 67, where Milton speaks of the Scriptures as " the just and adequate measure of truth . . . whose every part consenting, and making up the harmonious symmetry of complete instruction, is able to set out to us a perfect man of God." Cf. also the description of Christ in *P. L.* 3. 268-271.

verse about them, of Pythagoras who heard the music of the spheres, of Apollo and Orpheus who controlled the very stones, rivers, and trees of the inanimate world. It was thus that he imagined himself, a shepherd, singing " to the oaks and rills " which joined in the harmony of Nature as an accompaniment. To Milton the significance of music lies in its relation to the entire universe— to man first of all, to Nature as affecting man and possibly affected by him, and finally to God as controlling both Nature and man.

Paradise Lost is the work of a philosopher, a poet, and a Christian. Its inspiration may be found in that ideal of harmony which Milton expresses concretely in his conception of music. It is a description of the perfect harmony of the golden age of innocence, and of the discord caused by the intrusion of sin. "Man's first disobedience" upset the law and order of God. Figuratively, " discordant sin " ruined the musical harmony of the universe. The whole conception is summed up in the lines *At a Solemn Music*, which represent *Paradise Lost* in miniature. In spite of its pagan imagery, it is essentially a Christian prayer, that the " sphere-born harmonious sisters, Voice and Verse " may bring to our ears the celestial music of angel harps and trumpets,

> That we on Earth, with undiscording voice,
> May rightly answer that melodious noise,
> As once we did, till disproportioned Sin
> Jarred against Nature's chime, and with harsh din
> Broke the fair music that all creatures made
> To their great Lord, whose love their motion swayed
> In perfect diapason, whilst they stood
> In first obedience, and their state of good.
> O, may we soon again renew that song,
> And keep in tune with Heaven, till God ere long
> To his celestial consort us unite,
> To live with him, and sing in endless morn of light!

APPENDIX I

The most important Passages in Milton's Works, Illustrating his Knowledge of Music, arranged in chronological order, with comments.

1. *Elegy* 6. 39—46 (1626) :

> Auditurque chelys suspensa tapetia circum,
> Virgineos tremula quae regat arte pedes.
> Illa tuas saltem teneant spectacula Musas,
> Et revocent quantum crapula pellit iners.
> Crede mihi, dum psallit ebur,[1] comitataque plectrum
> Implet odoratos festa chorea tholos,
> Percipies tacitum per pectora serpere Phoebum,
> Quale repentinus permeat ossa calor.

2. *Nativity Hymn* 93—140 (1629) :

IX.

> When such music sweet
> Their hearts and ears did greet
> As never was by mortal finger strook,
> Divinely-warbled voice
> Answering the stringed noise,
> As all their souls in blissful rapture took :
> The air, such pleasure loth to lose,
> With thousand echoes still prolongs each heavenly close.

---

[1] *Dum psallit ebur.* Not the dancing of ivory keys, as interpreted by Cowper and Masson, but rather the strokes of the plectrum, with which the lyre was often played. The Greek term for playing a stringed instrument with a plectrum was ψάλλειν, as opposed to κρούειν, κρέκειν, πλήσσειν, " to play with the fingers," and there is little doubt that in this instance *psallit* means the same. In any case, Milton would hardly introduce a contemporary keyed instrument, such as the virginal, into such classical surroundings. Kircher, *Mus. Univ.* 2. 4. 1 applies the name *chelys* to instruments

X.

Nature, that heard such sound
Beneath the hollow round
Of Cynthia's seat, the airy region thrilling,[1]
Now was almost won
To think her part was done,
And that her reign had here its last fulfilling :
She knew such harmony alone
Could hold all Heaven and Earth in happier union.[2]

XI.

At last surrounds their sight
A globe of circular light,
That with long beams the shamefaced Night arrayed ;
The helmèd Cherubim
And sworded Seraphim
Are seen in glittering ranks with wings displayed,
Harping in loud and solemn quire,
With unexpressive notes, to Heaven's new-born Heir.[3]

---

of the viol family—*Quam vulgo viola gamba vocant*. But in this interpretation the *ebur* would again be meaningless. The *chelys* must be considered here in its classic significance, as an instrument of the lyre family. Milton probably has in mind the lute, which is to him the contemporary representative of the ancient lyre. Cf. *Ad Leonoram* 2. 6 ; *C.* 478.

[1] Cf. *De Sphaer. Con.*, below, Appendix IV, p. 134, 1. 19.

[2] The implication is that the laws of nature would be unnecessary if this harmony between Heaven and Earth could only continue indefinitely. It alone can effect a true union, such as once existed, before Sin entered into the world. Cf. st. XIV; *P. L.* 10. 656-719 ; and Spenser, *F. Q.* 5. 2. 34 ff.

[3] Professor Cook, *Trans. Conn. Acad.* 15. 341, notes that " at this point there seems to be no singing, but only harping." Such an interpretation is inconsistent with Milton's habit of using the harp only as an instrument of accompaniment. The word " quire " is here sufficient to suggest the song which the harps accompany. Moreover, there is nothing to indicate a cessation of the " divinely-warbled voice." The Cherubim and Seraphim, though not singing themselves, are accompanying the song of the rest of the angelic

XII.

Such music (as 'tis said)
Before was never made,
But when of old the Sons of Morning sung,
   While the Creator great
   His constellations set,
And the well-balanced world on hinges hung ;
And cast the dark foundations deep,
And bid the weltering waves their oozy channel keep.[1]

XIII.

Ring out, ye crystal spheres!
   Once bless our human ears,
   If ye have power to touch our senses so ; [2]
   And let your silver chime
   Move in melodious time,
   And let the bass of Heaven's deep organ blow ; [3]

host. The comparison at the beginning of stanza XII implies that
the song is still kept up. Cf. also " angelic symphony," l. 132, and
s. v. *symphony* (1) G.

[1] See below, *P. L.* 7. 253 ff. ; 275 ; 557 ff.

[2] Cf. *De Sphaer. Con.* below, Appendix IV, p. 134, l. 21.

[3] *The bass of Heaven's deep organ* may possibly be interpreted
literally, as Burnet would have it (*Early Greek Philosophy*, London,
1908, p. 351, n. 3), but it would seem that the bass is here not a following part but a leading one. Classical accounts of the musical scale
of the heavens varied, the lowest notes being assigned to the furthest
sphere by Nichomachus, and by Servius in his scholium on Virgil,
Aen. 2. 255, and to that of the moon by Cicero and Martianus
Capella. According to *A.* 72, and *S. M.* 23, Milton seems to
conceive of the sphere-music as having its highest notes in Heaven.
But he evidently concerned himself little with the exact details of
the system, being attracted chiefly by its poetical and ethical possibilities. Here he seems to be thinking of the fundamental or most
important tones as much as of actual bass notes. Himself an organist,
he naturally makes an organ the centre of his universal music. It
may be that he imagines Heaven's organ as sounding the " plain-
song " to which the spheres add their " descant." Cf. the abandoned
reading of *C.* 243 : " And hold a counterpoint to all Heaven's har-

And with your ninefold harmony
Make up full consort to the angelic symphony.[1]

XIV.

For, if such holy song
Enwrap our fancy long,
Time will run back, and fetch the Age of Gold[2] ;
And speckled Vanity
Will sicken soon and die,
And leprous Sin will melt from earthly mould ;
And Hell itself will pass away,
And leave her dolorous mansions to the peering day.

3. *The Passion* 22—28 (1630) :

These latest scenes confine my roving verse,
To this horizon is my Phoebus bound.
His godlike acts, and his temptations fierce,
And former sufferings, otherwhere are found,
Loud o'er the rest Cremona's trump[3] doth sound,
Me softer airs befit, and softer strings
Of lute or viol still, more apt for mournful things.

---

monies." Philo, *De Somn.* 1. 7. 37 calls Heaven the " arche-typum organum."

[1] The notion of the angels singing in harmony with the music of the spheres seems to be Neo-Platonic. Philo hints at such a conception, *De Somn.* 1. 6-7. Ambrosius states it very clearly. See the passage quoted in Appendix V, p. 145. Cf. also Dante, *Purg.* 30. 92-93.

[2] Cf. *De Sphaer. Con.* Appendix IV, p. 136, l. 3.

[3] *Cremona's trump* refers to Vida's *Christiad.* Warton (n. on p. 26) wrongly assumed that Milton considered this " the finest Latin poem on a religious subject." The comparison with the trumpet implies merely a noisy, proclamatory style. It is significant, too, that Milton contrasts with Vida his own " softer airs " and " softer strings "; cf. similar contrasts of gentle sounds with those of the trumpet, *P. L.* 11. 713 ; *H.* 58 ff. Milton's general use of the trumpet shows clearly that its actual sound is not pleasant to his ears. See reff. in G., esp. *P. L.* 6. 69 ; *P. R.* 1. 19, and cf. his sarcastic comment on the " trumpet of Salmasius," *P. W.* 1. 232.

4. *Ad Patrem* 17—29 (1630) :

> Nec tu, vatis opus, divinum despice carmen,
> Quo nihil aethereos ortus et semina coeli,
> Nil magis humanam commendat origine mentem,
> Sancta Prometheae retinens vestigia flammae.
> Carmen amant Superi, tremebundaque Tartara carmen
> Ima ciere valet, divosque ligare profundos,[1]
> Et triplici duros Manes ademante coercet.[2]
> Carmine sepositi retegunt arcana futuri
> Phoebades, et tremulae pallentes ora Sibyllae ;
> Carmina sacrificus sollennes pangit ad aras,
> Aurea seu sternit motantem cornua taurum,
> Seu cum fata sagax fumantibus abdita fibris
> Consulit, et tepidis Parcam scrutatur in extis.

Ad Patrem 30—40 [3] :

> Nos etiam, patrium tunc cum repetemus Olympum,
> Aeternaeque morae stabunt immobilis aevi,
> Ibimus auratis per coeli templa coronis,
> Dulcia suaviloquo sociantes carmina plectro,
> Astra quibus geminique poli convexa sonabunt
> Spiritus et rapidos qui circinat igneus orbes
> Nunc quoque sidereis intercinit ipse choreis
> Immortale melos et inenarrabile carmen,
> Torrida dum rutilus compescit sibila Serpens,[4]
> Demissoque ferox gladio mansuescit Orion,
> Stellarum nec sentit onus Maurusius Atlas.[5]

---

[1] Cf. *P. L.* 2. 552-555 ; *V. Ex.* 52 ; *L'A.* 149 ; *Il P.* 107-108.

[2] Cf. *A.* 65-66 ; 68-69.

[3] Here the Christian feelings of the *Solemn Music* are presented in pagan phraseology.

[4] Cf. the allusion to Delphinus, *De Sphaer. Con.* Appendix IV, p. 134, l. 2.

[5] Cf. the allusion to Atlas, " panting and sweating under his burden," *De Sphaer. Con.* Appendix IV, p. 133, l. 26.

Ad Patrem 50—55 [1] :

Denique quid vocis modulamen inane juvabit,
Verborum sensusque vacans, numerique loquacis ?
Silvestres decet iste choros, non Orphea, cantus,
Qui tenuit fluvios, et quercubus addidit aures,
Carmine, non cithara, simulacraque functa canendo
Compulit in lacrymas ; habet has a carmine laudes.

Ad Patrem 56—66 :

Nec tu perge, precor, sacras contemnere Musas,
Nec vanas inopesque puta, quarum ipse peritus
Munere mille sonos numeros componis ad aptos,
Millibus et vocem modulis variare canoram
Doctus, Arionii merito sis nominis haeres.
Nunc tibi quid mirum, si me genuisse poetam
Contigerit, charo si tam prope sanguine juncti
Cognatas artes, studiumque affine, sequamur ?
Ipse volens Phoebus se dispertire duobus,
Altera dona mihi, dedit altera dona parenti ;
Dividuumque Deum, genitorque puerque, tenemus.

5. *L'Allegro* 135—144 (1632—33) :

And ever, against eating cares,
Lap me in soft Lydian airs,
Married to immortal verse,
Such as the meeting soul may pierce,
In notes with many a winding bout
Of linkèd sweetness long drawn out,
With wanton heed, and giddy cunning,
The melting voice [2] through mazes running,

[1] Cf. the description of Apollo's song, *Ad Mansum* 54-69, and see pp. 98, 99.

[2] With this visionary singer cf. the visionary organist of *P. L.* 11. 561 ff. The same delight in an orderly confusion of sounds is here evident. The singer is evidently so well-trained as to make his accuracy (heed) seem careless (wanton), and his scientific skill (cunning) a matter of mere recklessness (giddy). Similarly, in *P. L.* 5. 623-624, the mazes of the celestial dance are

Untwisting all the chains that tie
The hidden soul of harmony.[1]

6. *Il Penseroso* 161—166 (1632—33) :

There let the pealing organ blow
To the full-voiced quire below,
In service high and anthems clear,
As may with sweetness, through mine ear,
Dissolve me into ecstasies,
And bring all Heaven before mine eyes.[2]

7. *Sonnet, To the Nightingale* (1633) :

O Nightingale, that on yon bloomy spray
    Warblest [3] at eve, when all the woods are still,
    Thou with fresh hope the lover's heart dost fill,
    While the jolly Hours lead [4] on propitious May ;

                                    regular
            Then most when most irregular they seem.
Yet all this seemingly careless confusion, these brilliant runs and
baffling combinations of notes, are really controlled by a definite
system. It is only by solving these problems that the real soul
of harmony is reached. Milton may well have had in mind compositions such as those of Monteverde, in which brilliant runs were
a feature. Cf. the specimen in Hawkins 3. 436-438. " O had I
wings," by Milton's father, shows some intricate " mazes." See
Hawkins 3. 369-371.

    [1] Cf. *De Sphaer. Con.* Appendix IV, p. 134, l. 14 ; *P. L.* 5. 625-627.
Cf. also Pherecrates' description of the binding of Μουσική by Timotheus of Miletus, Plutarch, *De Musica* 30.
    [2] Cf. *V. Ex.* 32-38 :
        Before thou clothe my fancy in fit sound :
        Such where the deep transported mind may soar
        Above the wheeling poles, and at Heaven's door
        Look in, and see each blissful deity
        How he before the thunderous throne doth lie,
        Listening to what unshorn Apollo sings
        To the touch of golden wires.
    [3] G., s. v. *warble.*
    [4] *Lead*, i. e., in dance ; cf. *P. L.* 4. 268.

Thy liquid notes that close the eye of day,
   First heard before the shallow cuckoo's bill,
   Portend success in love. O if Jove's will
Have linked that amorous power to thy soft lay,[1]
Now timely sing, ere the rude bird of hate
   Foretell my hopeless doom, in some grove nigh;
   As thou from year to year hast sung too late
For my relief, yet hadst no reason why.
   Whether the Muse or Love call thee his mate,
   Both them I serve, and of their train am I.

8. *Arcades* 61—73 (1633—34) :

But else in deep of night when drowsiness
Hath locked up mortal sense, then listen I
To the celestial Sirens' harmony,[2]
That sit upon the nine enfolded spheres,
And sing to those that hold the vital shears,
And turn the adamantine spindle round,
On which the fate of gods and men is wound.
Such sweet compulsion doth in music lie,
To lull the daughters of Necessity,
And keep unsteady Nature to her law,
And the low world in measured motion draw
After the heavenly tune, which none can hear
Of human mould with gross unpurgèd ear.

[1] For the amorous character of the nightingale's song, cf. *P. L.* 4. 603 ; 771 ; 7. 436 ; 8. 518 ; *C.* 234.

[2] See below Appendix V, p. 144. In *S. M.* 1-2, the " blest pair of Sirens . . . sphere-born harmonious sisters, Voice and Verse " are thought of in the same way. In *C.* 241, Echo is " Daughter of the Sphere," and the promise that she shall " give resounding grace to all Heaven's harmonies " (243) indicates that she is one of the Sirens of the spheres. In *P. W.* 2. 481 Milton apparently identifies the nine celestial Sirens with the nine Muses when he speaks of " dame Memory and her siren daughters." See Martianus Capella, *De Nupt. Phil.* 1. 27-28, below, Appendix V, p. 146.

9. *At a Solemn Music* [1] (1633—34) :

Blest pair of Sirens, pledges of Heaven's joy,
Sphere-born harmonious sisters, Voice and Verse,
Wed your divine sounds, and mixed power employ
Dead things with inbreathed sense able to pierce ;
And to our high-raised phantasy present
That undisturbèd song of pure concent, [2]
Aye sung before the sapphire-coloured throne
To Him that sits thereon,
With saintly shout, and solemn jubilee ;
Where the bright Seraphim in burning row
Their loud uplifted angel-trumpets blow,
And the cherubic host in thousand quires
Touch their immortal harps of golden wires,
With those just Spirits that wear victorious palms,
Hymns devout and holy psalms
Singing everlastingly :
That we on Earth, with undiscording voice,
May rightly answer that melodious noise ;
As once we did, till disproportioned Sin
Jarred against Nature's chime, and with harsh din

[1] These lines are the highest and most perfect expression of
Milton's doctrine of a universal harmony. They are crowded with
metaphysical ideas, mystical Christianity, pagan mythology, and
technical terms of music. The opening is distinctly pagan, Voice
and Verse, i. e., the music and the words in song, being represented
as " daughters of the sphere," probably an echo of Neo-Platonism.
The celestial concert which follows is a combination of Plato's
sphere-music and the angelic song of Revelation. Cf. Plato,
Republic 10. 617 ; Revelation 14. 3.

[2] *Concent*: concord. In *Il P.* 93-96, Milton speaks of
those daemons that are found
In fire, air, flood, or underground,
Whose power hath a true consent
With planet, or with element.

Cf. *P. W.* 3. 67, " whose every part consenting, and making up
the harmonious symmetry," etc. In both cases the musical significance of " concent " seems to be lurking in his mind, although
there is no etymological connection with " consent."

Broke the fair music that all creatures made
To their great Lord, whose love their motion swayed
In perfect diapason,[1] whilst they stood
In first obedience, and their state of good.
O, may we soon again renew that song,
And keep in tune with Heaven, till God ere long
To his celestial consort [2] us unite,
To live with Him, and sing in endless morn of light !

10. *Comus* 543—562 [3] (1634) :

I sat me down to watch upon a bank
With ivy canopied, and interwove
With flaunting honeysuckle ; and began,
Wrapt in a pleasing fit of melancholy,
To meditate my rural minstrelsy
Till fancy had her fill ; but ere a close,
The wonted roar was up amidst the woods,
And filled the air with barbarous dissonance ;
At which I ceased, and listened them a while,
Till an unusual stop of sudden silence
Gave respite to the drowsy frighted steeds
That draw the litter of close-curtained Sleep.
At least a soft and solemn-breathing sound
Rose like a stream of rich distilled perfumes,
And stole upon the air, that even Silence
Was took ere she was ware, and wished she might
Deny her nature, and be never more,
Still to be so displaced. I was all ear,

---

[1] *Diapason* represents the harmony between Heaven and Earth as consisting of the interval of the octave, in other words, the most perfect concord excepting an actual unison. See p. 74. Man's state of good consisted in an undeviating conformity to divine law. Cf. above pp. 96-97.

[2] Either the music of the celestial choirs, or the choirs themselves. Cf. " Coelestium consortio," *De Sphaer. Con.* Appendix IV, p. 135, l. 7.

[3] The allusions to Harry Lawes in *Comus* and the *Sonnet* addressed to him (1645) are quoted in Appendix II.

And took in strains that might create a soul
Under the ribs of Death.

11. *Lycidas* 32—36 (1637) :

Meanwhile the rural ditties were not mute,
Tempered to the oaten flute ;
Rough Satyrs danced, and Fauns with cloven heel
From the glad sound would not be absent long ;
And old Damoetas loved to hear our song.

Lycidas 58—63 :

What could the Muse herself that Orpheus bore,
The Muse herself, for her enchanting son
Whom universal Nature did lament,
When by the rout that made the hideous roar,
His gory visage down the stream was sent,
Down the swift Hebrus to the Lesbian shore ?

Lycidas 172—180 :

So Lycidas sunk low, but mounted high,
Through the dear might of Him that walked the waves,
Where, other groves and other streams along,
With nectar pure his oozy locks he laves,
And hears the unexpressive nuptial song,
In the blest kingdoms meek of joy and love.
There entertain him all the Saints above,
In solemn troops and sweet societies,
That sing, and singing in their glory move.

Lycidas 186—189 :

Thus sang the uncouth swain to the oaks and rills,
While the still morn went out with sandals gray ;
He touched the tender stops of various quills,
With eager thought warbling his Doric lay.

12. *Three Latin Epigrams to Leonora Baroni, the Singer*
(1638—39). Quoted in Appendix III, pp. 129—130.

13. *Epitaphium Damonis* 215—219 (1639—40) :

> Ipse, caput nitidum cinctus rutilante corona,
> Laetaque frondentis gestans umbracula pa!mae,
> Aeternum perages immortales hymenaeos,
> Cantus ubi, choreisque furit lyra mista beatis
> Festa Sionaeo bacchantur et Orgia thyrso.

14. *Of Reformation in England, P. W.* 2. 418 (1641) :

Then, amidst the hymns and hallelujahs of saints, some one may perhaps be heard offering at high strains in new and lofty measure to sing and celebrate thy divine mercies and marvellous judgments in this land throughout all ages.

15. *Animadversions, P. W.* 2. 61—62 (1641) :

Variety (as both music and rhetoric teacheth us) erects and rouses an auditory, like the masterful running over many chords and divisions ; whereas if men should ever be thumbing the drone of one plain-song, it would be a dull opiate to the most wakeful attention.

16. *Tractate on Education, P. W.* 3. 476 (1644) :

The interim of unsweating themselves regularly, and convenient rest before meat, may, both with profit and delight, be taken up in recreating and composing their travailed spirits with the solemn and divine harmonies of music, heard or learned, either whilst the skilful organist plies his grave and fancied descant in lofty fugues, or the whole symphony with artful and unimaginable touches adorn and grace the well-studied chords of some choice composer ; sometimes the lute or soft organ-stop waiting on elegant voices, either to religious, martial, or civil ditties ; which, if wise men and prophets be not extremely out, have a great power over dispositions and manners, to smoothe and make them gentle from rustic harshness and distempered passions.[1]

---

[1] Cf. this actual organist with the visionary Jubal (*P. L.* 11. 562, below p. 121) pursuing his themes through all proportions low and high. When *grave*, the descant or improvisation may be said

17. *Areopagitica*, P. W. 2. 73 (1644) :

If we think to regulate printing, thereby to rectify manners, we must regulate all recreations and pastimes, all that is delightful to man. No music must be heard, no song be set or sung, but what is grave and doric. There must be licensing dancers, that no gesture, motion, or deportment be taught our youth, but what by their allowance shall be thought honest ; for such Plato was provided of. It will ask more than the work of twenty licensers to examine all the lutes, the violins, and the guitars in every house ; they must not be suffered to prattle as they do, but must be licensed what they may say. And who shall silence all the airs and madrigals that whisper softness in chambers ? The windows also, and the balconies, must be thought on ; these are shrewd books, with dangerous frontispieces, set to sale ; who shall prohibit them, shall twenty licensers ? The villages also must have their visitors to inquire what lectures the bagpipe and the rebeck reads, even to the ballatry and the gamut of every municipal fiddler ; for these are the countryman's Arcadias, and his Monte Mayors.[1]

to be in low proportions, but when *fancied* (i. e., fanciful), the proportions would become complex or high. The improvisation of the organist is compared with the performance of the well-studied chords of some choice composer by the entire company. Milton's intention, obviously, is to show how the boys themselves may take part in the music. He speaks above of the " divine harmonies of music heard or learned." Here, then, the pupils are represented as playing together, or singing, at times *a cappella*, at times with the accompaniment of lute or organ. The " artful and unimaginable touches " are in contrast with the natural descant of the organist. Formal set music is here compared with spontaneous improvisation.

[1] This sustained piece of sarcasm shows how naturally music came into Milton's mind, even in his bitterest controversial pamphlets. The reference to Plato seems to be based chiefly upon the *Laws* 2. 654 ; 655. The *ballatry* and *gamut* imply a limited and aimless style of music with little meaning (see G). Such poor, insignificant music, says Milton, is all the " literature " that a countryman possesses. Hence, why not license even it ?

18. *Sonnet* 13 (1645). Quoted in Appendix II, p. 124.

19. *P. L.* 1. 549—562 (1658—65) :

> Anon they move
> In perfect phalanx to the Dorian mood
> Of flutes and soft recorders—such as raised
> To highth of noblest temper heroes old
> Arming to battle, and instead of rage
> Deliberate valour breathed, firm and unmoved
> With dread of death to flight or foul retreat ;
> Nor wanting power to mitigate and swage
> With solemn touches troubled thoughts, and chase
> Anguish and doubt and fear and sorrow and pain
> From mortal or immortal minds. Thus they,
> Breathing united force with fixèd thought,
> Moved on in silence, to soft pipes that charmed
> Their painful steps o'er the burnt soil.[1]

P. L. 1. 705—709 :

> A third as soon had formed within the ground
> A various mould, and from the boiling cells
> By strange conveyance filled each hollow nook,
> As in an organ, from one blast of wind,
> To many a row of pipes the sound-board breathes.[2]

P. L. 2. 284—290 :

> He scarce had finished, when such murmur filled
> The assembly, as when hollow rocks retain
> The sound of blustering winds, which all night long
> Had roused the sea, now with hoarse cadence[3] lull

[1] This is Milton's clearest exposition of the ἦθος of the Dorian mode. It was evidently his favorite, as it was Plato's. Cf. *Laches* 188 D ; *Republic* 3. 399. See G., and cf. pp. 66, 67.

[2] See Prof. Edward Taylor's explanation of this simile, quoted by Keightley, *Life*, p. 433.

[3] The " hoarse cadence " represents the gradual *diminuendo* of the music of the winds, which, stored up in the hollow rocks as in the wind-chest of an organ, breathe their lullaby even after the

Sea-faring men o'er-watched, whose bark by chance,
Or pinnace, anchors in a craggy bay
After the tempest.

P. L. 2. 546—555 :

     Others, more mild,
Retreated in a silent valley, sing
With notes angelical to many a harp
Their own heroic deeds and hapless fall
By doom of battle ; and complain that Fate
Free Virtue should enthral to Force or Chance.
Their song was partial,[1] but the harmony
(What could it less when spirits immortal sing ?)
Suspended Hell, and took with ravishment
The thronging audience.

P. L. 3. 26—40 :

     Yet not the more
Cease I to wander where the Muses haunt
Clear spring, or shady grove, or sunny hill,
Smit with the love of sacred song ; but chief
Thee, Sion, and the flowery brooks beneath,
That wash thy hallowed feet, and warbling flow,
Nightly I visit ; nor sometimes forget
Those other two equalled with me in fate,
So were I equalled with them in renown,
Blind Thamyris and blind Maeonides,

commotion of the tempest has ceased. The figure is fanciful, yet
well sustained and full of beauty.

[1] The fallen angels, similar to the angels in Heaven, instinctively
sing in harmony, even though their song is *partial*, i. e., scattered,
each one singing for himself alone, without true concent. As usual,
Milton is playing on the meaning of a word, using " partial " not
only in contrast with " harmony," in a musical sense, but also
as suggesting the pride and selfishness of the fallen angels. The
perfect harmony of Heaven has been disturbed and lost in their
case, but enough is left to ravish Hell, in spite of its " par-
tiality," both musical and mental.

And Tiresias and Phineus, prophets old :
Then feed on thoughts that voluntary move
Harmonious numbers ; as the wakeful bird
Sings darkling, and, in shadiest covert hid,
Tunes her nocturnal note.

P. L. 3. 344–349 ; 365–371 :

No sooner had the Almighty ceased, but—all
The multitude of angels, with a shout
Loud as from numbers without number, sweet
As from blest voices, uttering joy—Heaven rung
With jubilee, and loud hosannas filled
The eternal regions.
. . . .
Then, crowned again, their golden harps they took,
Harps ever tuned, that glittering by their side
Like quivers hung ; and with preamble sweet
Of charming symphony they introduce
Their sacred song, and waken raptures high ;
No voice exempt, no voice but well could join
Melodious part ; such concord is in Heaven.

P. L. 3. 579–582 :

They, as they move
Their starry dance in numbers that compute
Days, months, and years, towards his all-cheering lamp
Turn swift their various motions.

P. L. 4. 264–268 :

The birds their quire apply ; airs, vernal airs,
Breathing the smell of field and grove, attune
The trembling leaves, while universal Pan
Knit with the Graces and the Hours in dance
Led on the eternal Spring.

P. L. 4. 601—603 :

> They to their grassy couch, these to their nests
> Were slunk, all but the wakeful nightingale ;
> She all night long her amorous descant [1] sung.

P. L. 4. 675—688 :

>   Nor think, though men were none,
> That Heaven would want spectators, God want praise.
> Millions of spiritual creatures walk the earth
> Unseen, both when we wake, and when we sleep :
> All these with ceaseless praise his works behold,
> Both day and night.   How often, from the steep
> Of echoing hill or thicket, have we heard
> Celestial voices to the midnight air,
> Sole, or responsive each to other's note
> Singing their great Creator !   Oft in bands
> While they keep watch, or nightly rounding walk,
> With heavenly touch of instrumental sounds
> In full harmonic number joined, their songs
> Divide the night, and lift our thoughts to Heaven.

P. L. 5. 144—204 :

> Lowly they bowed, adoring, and began
> Their orisons, each morning duly paid
> In various style ; for neither various style
> Nor holy rapture wanted they to praise
> Their Maker, in fit strains pronounced or sung
> Unmeditated ; such prompt eloquence

---

[1] As *descant* implies improvisation on a set theme, Milton must have in mind something of the nature of a plain-song, which the nightingale accompanies. Possibly he intends to picture two or more nightingales, singing alternately or in harmony, the one a plain-song, the other a descant. Cf. 1. 771 :

>   These, lulled by nightingales, embracing slept.

More probably, however, it is the music of Nature which supplies the plain-song to which the nightingale extemporizes its variations. Cf. *De Sphaer. Con.* below, Appendix IV, p. 134, l. 7 ; *L.* 186.

Flowed from their lips, in prose or numerous verse,
More tuneable than needed lute or harp
To add more sweetness ; and they thus began :
   " These are thy glorious works, Parent of good,
Almighty ! thine this universal frame,
Thus wondrous fair : thyself how wondrous then !
Unspeakable ! who sitt'st above these Heavens
To us invisible, or dimly seen
In these thy lowest works ; yet these declare
Thy goodness beyond thought, and power divine.[1]
Speak, ye who best can tell, ye Sons of Light,
Angels—for ye behold him, and with songs
And choral symphonies, day without night,
Circle his throne rejoicing—ye in Heaven ;
On earth join all ye creatures, to extol
Him first, him last, him midst, and without end.
Fairest of stars, last in the train of night,
If better thou belong not to the dawn,
Sure pledge of day, that crown'st the smiling morn
With thy bright circlet, praise him in thy sphere
While day arises, that sweet hour of prime.
Thou Sun, of this great world both eye and soul,
Acknowledge him thy greater, sound his praise
In thy eternal course, both when thou climb'st,
And when high noon hast gained, and when thou
   fall'st.
Moon, that now meet'st the orient Sun, now fliest,
With the fixed stars, fixed in their orb that flies,
And ye five other wandering Fires, that move
In mystic dance, not without song, resound
His praise who out of darkness called up light.
Air, and ye Elements, the eldest birth
Of Nature's womb, that in quaternion run

---

[1] In describing this universal music Milton gradually descends
from Heaven itself through the various spheres to the earth and the
forces of Nature. Criticism of the accuracy of the system is unnecessary, for the conception is frankly poetical. Cf. Spenser, *F. Q.* 2.
12. 33 ; 70-71 ; Tasso, *G. L.* 16. 12 ; and see above, pp. 77-78.

Perpetual circle, multiform. and mix
And nourish all things, let your ceaseless change
Vary to our great Maker still new praise.
Ye Mists and Exhalations that now rise
From hill or steaming lake, dusky or gray,
Till the sun paint your fleecy skirts with gold,
In honour to the world's great Author rise,
Whether to deck with clouds the uncoloured sky,
Or wet the thirsty earth with falling showers,
Rising or falling, still advance his praise.
His praise, ye Winds, that from four quarters blow,
Breathe soft or loud ; and wave your tops, ye Pines,
With every plant, in sign of worship wave.
Fountains, and ye that warble, as ye flow,
Melodious murmurs, warbling tune his praise.
Join voices all ye living Souls ; ye Birds,
That singing up to Heaven-gate ascend,
Bear on your wings and in your notes his praise.
Ye that in waters glide, and ye that walk
The earth, and stately tread, or lowly creep,
Witness if I be silent, morn or even,
To hill or valley, fountain, or fresh shade,
Made vocal by my song, and taught his praise.

P. L. 5. 618—627 :

That day, as other solemn days, they spent
In song and dance about the sacred hill,
Mystical dance, which yonder starry sphere
Of planets and of fixed in all her wheels
Resembles nearest ; mazes intricate,[1]
Eccentric, intervolved, yet regular
Then most when most irregular they seem,
And in their motions Harmony divine [2]
So smoothes her charming tones, that God's own ear
Listens delighted.

[1] Cf. Plato, *Timaeus* 40. (Quoted below, Appendix V, p. 144.)
[2] The personified Harmony seems to be a reminiscence of Plato's
Sirens, *Rep.* 10. 617, and of their adaptation in *S. M.* 8.

P. L. 6. 59—68 :

Nor with less dread the loud

Ethereal trumpet from on high gan blow :
At which command the powers militant,
That stood for Heaven, in mighty quadrate joined
Of union irresistible, moved on
In silence their bright legions, to the sound
Of instrumental harmony,[1] that breathed
Heroic ardor to adventurous deeds
Under their god-like leaders, in the cause
Of God and his Messiah.

P. L. 7. 30—38 :

Still govern thou my song,

Urania, and fit audience find, though few.
But drive far off the barbarous dissonance
Of Bacchus and his revellers, the race
Of that wild rout that tore the Thraçian bard
In Rhodope, where woods and rocks had ears
To rapture, till the savage clamour drowned
Both harp and voice ; nor could the Muse defend
Her son.

P. L. 7. 252—260 :

Thus was the first day even and morn;

Nor past uncelebrated, nor unsung
By the celestial quires, when orient light
Exhaling first from darkness they beheld,
Birth-day of Heaven and earth ; with joy and shout
The hollow universal orb they filled,
And touched their golden harps, and hymning praised
God and his works ; Creator him they sung,
Both when first evening was, and when first morn.

---

[1] The *instrumental harmony* was probably in the Dorian mode, similar to that of the " flutes and soft recorders " of *P. L.* 1. 554.

P. L. 7. 433—436 :

> From branch to branch the smaller birds with song
> Solaced the woods, and spread their painted wings
> Till even ; nor then the solemn nightingale
> Ceased warbling, but all night tuned her soft lays.

P. L. 7. 557—565 :

> Up he rode,
> Followed with acclamation and the sound
> Symphonious of ten thousand harps that tuned
> Angelic harmonies. The earth, the air
> Resounded (thou remember'st, for thou heard'st)
> The heavens and all the constellations rung,
> The planets in their stations listening stood,
> While the bright pomp ascended jubilant.
> " Open, ye everlasting gates ! " they sung.

P. L. 7. 594—599 :

> The harp
> Had work and rested not, the solemn pipe
> And dulcimer, all organs of sweet stop,
> All sounds on fret by string or golden wire,
> Tempered soft tunings, intermixed with voice
> Choral or unison.

P. L. 8. 261—266 :

> About me round I saw
> Hill, dale, and shady woods, and sunny plains,
> And liquid lapse of murmuring streams ; by these,
> Creatures that lived and moved, and walked or flew,
> Birds on the branches warbling ; all things smiled,
> With fragrance and with joy my heart o'erflowed.

P. L. 8. 513—520 :

> The earth
> Gave sign of gratulation, and each hill ;
> Joyous the birds ; fresh gales and gentle airs
> Whispered it to the woods, and from their wings

Flung rose, flung odours from the spicy shrub,
Disporting, till the amorous bird of night
Sung spousal, and bid haste the evening star
On his hill-top, to light the bridal lamp.

P. L. 11. 556—563 :

He looked, and saw a spacious plain, whereon
Were tents of various hue ; by some were herds
Of cattle grazing ; others whence the sound
Of instruments that made melodious chime
Was heard, of harp and organ ; and who moved
Their stops and chords was seen[1] ; his volant touch
Instinct, through all proportions low and high
Fled and pursued transverse the resonant fugue.

19. *P. R.* 2. 354—365 (1671) :

Under the trees now tripped, now solemn stood
Nymphs of Diana's train, and Naiades

---

[1] The visionary organist is Jubal, " the father of all such as
handle the harp and organ " (Genesis 4. 21). Milton builds up from
this slight Scriptural hint, by his technical knowledge of organ-
playing, a picture of the greatest complexity, yet accurate in every
detail. The organist is evidently improvising, with volant, i. e.,
light, flying touch. *Instinct* does not necessarily mean " instinctively."
Milton probably has the Latin *instinctus* in mind and intends to
express the divine inspiration which governs the musician's touch.
The *proportions*, or mathematical relations of the music, are *low*
and *high* not as differing in pitch but in complexity. Simple intervals or rhythms are naturally termed *low*. Conversely, the more
complex proportions are *high*. Cf. the table in *Morley*, p. 38, and
see above, Appendix I, p. 111, n. The word-order, " low and high,"
seems inconsistent with a conventional reference to variations of
pitch. The organist chases his themes back and forth (*transverse*)
through the intricate fugue structure, sounding them again and
again (*resonant*). Milton's fugue was not, of course, of the construction which we find perfected in Bach. It was chiefly in strict
canon. In the so-called " unlimited fugue," considerable freedom
of invention was possible. It was this style, as developed by Frescobaldi, that Milton probably had in mind.

With fruits and flowers from Amalthea's horn,
And ladies of the Hesperides, that seemed
Fairer than feigned of old, or fabled since
Of fairy damsels met in forest wide
By knights of Logres, or of Lyones,
Lancelot, or Pelleas, or Pellenore.
And all the while harmonious airs were heard
Of chiming strings or charming pipes, and winds
Of gentlest gale Arabian odours fanned
From their soft wings, and Flora's earliest smells.[1]

P. R. 4. 244—260 :

See there the olive-grove of Academe,
Plato's retirement, where the Attic bird
Trills her thick-warbled notes the summer long ;
There flowery hill Hymettus, with the sound
Of bees' industrious murmur, oft invites
To studious musing ; there Ilissus rolls
His whispering stream ; within the walls then view
The schools of ancient sages—his who bred
Great Alexander to subdue the world,
Lyceum there, and painted Stoa next :
[2] There shalt thou hear and learn the secret power
Of harmony, in tones and numbers [3] hit
By voice or hand ; and various-measured verse,
Aeolian charms and Dorian lyric odes,
And his, who gave them breath, but higher sung,
Blind Melesigenes thence Homer called,
Whose poem Phoebus challenged for his own.

[1] The description of these tempting delights may have been suggested by Spenser's enchanted bower, *F. Q.* 2. 12. 70-71.

[2] Milton connects the study of music most naturally with the schools of philosophy. His own theory of music was largely derived from those sources.

[3] *Tones* and *numbers* are constrasted as representing the art and the theory of music. Both phases were prominent in the culture of ancient Greece. Possibly Milton also has in mind the contrast between variation of pitch (tones) and rhythm (numbers as the two elements in melody).

19. *S. A.* 206—209 (1671) :

> Immeasurable strength they might behold
> In me, of wisdom nothing more than mean ;
> This with the other should, at least, have paired ;
> These two, proportioned ill, drove me transverse.[1]

---

[1] A distinct musical metaphor is contained in these lines. They have usually been explained as a continuation of the metaphor of a ship occurring eight lines above. This explanation is based entirely on the words *drove me transverse*, which are compared with *P. L.* 4. 488. But the rest of the passage has no meaning when applied to a ship. On the other hand the word *transverse* is used in *P. L.* 11. 563 in a distinctly musical sense. This, with the reference to *proportion*, seems to indicate a musical meaning here. If the life of Samson is compared with a piece of music in which the harmony of the theme has been disturbed, the whole metaphor becomes clear. In the construction of this musical composition, *strength*, the dominant note, was *immeasurable*. Wisdom, which should have harmonized with it, was only moderate. Possibly Milton intended a pun on the word *mean*, which in music represents a middle note, completing a triad. If strength and wisdom could not harmonize, in the sense of a concord of two different notes, they *should, at least, have paired*, that is, sounded in unison. But, being *proportioned ill*, that is, incorrect in their relationship, they upset the harmony of the entire composition. It is by no means an unusual type of figure in Milton, for he is fond of playing upon the Platonic conception of the soul of man as a harmony. Cf. Shakespeare's " sweet bells jangled out of time and harsh."

APPENDIX II

MILTON'S FRIENDSHIP WITH HENRY LAWES,
THE COMPOSER

Sonnet XIII.

To my friend Mr. Henry Lawes.

Harry, whose tuneful and well-measured song
First taught our English music how to span
Words with just note and accent, not to scan
With Midas' ears, committing short and long ;
Thy worth and skill exempts thee from the throng,
With praise enough for envy to look wan ;
To after age thou shalt be writ the man
That with smooth air couldst humor best our tongue.
Thou honour'st Verse, and Verse must lend her wing
To honour thee, the priest of Phoebus' quire,
That tun'st their happiest lines in hymn or story.
Dante shall give Fame leave to set thee higher
Than his Casella, whom he wooed to sing,
Met in the milder shades of Purgatory.

The allusions to Lawes in *Comus*:

. . . But first I must put off
These my sky-robes, spun out of Iris' woof,
And take the weeds and likeness of a swain
That to the service of this house belongs[1] ;

---

[1] Lines 84-88 of the *Comus* refer to Lawes' connection with the Earl of Bridgewater's family. As music-teacher he could be said to belong " to the service of this house." The implied comparison with Apollo and Orpheus, whose music exerted a power even over the forces of Nature, is the highest compliment of which Milton is capable. A similar compliment is given in lines 494-496 (cf. also 623 ff.). The reference to " his madrigal " should be taken literally as denoting a style of music in which Lawes was well versed, not

Who, with, his soft pipe and smooth-dittied song,
Well knows to still the wild winds when they roar,

merely as " pastoral song." In staging the *Comus*, Lawes took
some liberties with Milton's text. He used a portion of the epi-
logue, with slight changes, as an opening song, beginning " From
the heavens now I fly." It appears thus in the Bridgewater MS.
In the song *Sweet Echo*, a line of Milton's first draft, " and hold a
counterpoint to all Heaven's harmonies," was retained instead
of the revision " and give resounding grace to all Heaven's harmonies." Hawkins evidently thought that Lawes had made this
change to a more technical term, and called it " a quaint alteration
of the reading . . . which none but a musician would have thought
of."—Hawkins 4. 52. He is quite right in the latter remark, but the
musician was Milton himself, not Lawes.

The music of *Sweet Echo* is printed by both Hawkins (3. 53)
and Burney (3. 383) as a good example of Lawes' style. *Back
Shepherds* and a quotation from *Sabrina Fair* may be found in
the *Oxford History of Music* 3. 203. Only five songs are known,
the other two being *From the heavens* and *Now my task*. These
five songs are in the British Museum, *Add. MSS*. 11. 518, and
were published by the Mermaid Society in 1904. They cannot
have constituted the entire music of the masque, for the stage
directions call for a " measure ", or dance of Comus' rabble, and
for "soft music " preceding line 659. Sabrina, also, after line
889, "rises . . . and sings ". The song *Back Shepherds* should
be followed by "a second song ". All this music has evidently
been lost.

The sonnet to Henry Lawes was dated by Milton himself, Feb. 9,
1645. Two copies in the author's own hand may be found in the
Cambridge Facsimile. In these the title stands as above. The
sonnet was prefixed by Lawes in 1648 to the *Choice Psalms*, the
same title being used. But in the edition of 1673 of Milton's Poems
the sonnet was called " To Mr. Henry Lawes on his Airs." This
title, with a variation " To Mr. H. Lawes on the publishing his
Airs," has been wrongly retained in subsequent editions, and has
given rise to a very natural misunderstanding. It has been re-
marked that the sonnet appears only before the *Psalms* of Lawes,
and not before the *Airs* of later date. See the discussion in *Notes
and Queries*, 2nd Ser. 9. 337 ; 395 ; 492. Assuming that the title " On
the publishing his Airs " was Milton's own, it has been argued that
Lawes must have intended to publish his airs in 1645, but put it

And hush the waving woods . . .

                                        82—88.

Thyrsis ! Whose artful strains have oft delayed

off because of the unfavorable state of the times, and possibly also because of the death of his brother ; and that he used the sonnet for the *Psalms* in 1648, suppressing part of the title. This argument, of course, has no weight, since Milton's own title is shown by his MS. to be " To my friend Mr. Henry Lawes." The question of the poet's real intentions in writing the sonnet, however, is an interesting one. A marginal note in the *Choice Psalms* tells us that " story " (*Son.* 13. 11) refers to " the story of Ariadne set by him to music." Now, the Story of Theseus and Ariadne is the first piece in the first book of *Airs*, 1653, and is particularly noticed by several of the writers of commendatory verses prefixed to that collection. If the marginal note of the *Choice Psalms* tells the truth, then, either Milton did intend the *Sonnet* for the actual *Airs*, or else he was familiar with *Theseus and Ariadne* in MS.form. Either conclusion is interesting. For in both cases some light is thrown upon the intimacy of the poet and the musician. It is perhaps safest to decide that the sonnet was a mere private expression of friendship, and that it was used by Lawes in his next publication, with the permission of the author.

The real interest of the sonnet lies in the opinion which Milton expresses of the music of Lawes. Is it to be considered the exaggerated and unreasonable praise of a friend, or the critical comment of a scholarly musician ? Musical historians, on the whole, are not inclined to agree with Milton. Burney says : " The notes set by Lawes to the song of *Sweet Echo* neither constitute an air, nor melody ; and, indeed, they are even too frequently prolonged for recitative. It is difficult to give a name, from the copious technica with which the art of Music is furnished, to such a series of unmeaning sounds. Nor does the composer, otherwise than comparatively, seem to merit the great praises bestowed upon him by Milton and others for his ' exact accommodation of the accent of the music and the quantities of the verse,' which perhaps, without a very nice examination, has been granted to him by late writers. As no accompaniment, but a dry bass, seems to have been given to this song by the composer, it is difficult to imagine how the Lady was able

                    ' to wake the courteous Echo
            To give an answer from her mossy couch.'

The huddling brook to hear his madrigal,
And sweetened every musk-rose of the dale.
494—496.

Here was a favorable opportunity suggested to the musician for
instrumental ritornales and iterations, of which, however, he made
no use." (Burney 3. 382). After quoting the song, *Sweet Echo,*
entire, Burney proceeds to point out half a dozen " inaccuracies
of musical accentuation," which seem to him " indefensible." Moreover he finds that " the interval from F sharp to E natural, the
seventh above, is certainly one of the most disagreeable notes in
melody that the scale could furnish. I should be glad, indeed,"
he concludes, " to be informed by the most exclusive admirer of
old ditties, what is the musical merit of this song, except insipid
simplicity, and its having been set for a single voice, instead of
being mangled by the many-headed monster, Madrigal ? " (*Ibid.*
3. 384). Later he says, " I have examined with care and candor all
the works I can find of this composer , which are still very numerous,
and am obliged to own myself unable, by their excellence, to account
for the great reputation he acquired, and the numerous panegyrics
bestowed upon him by the greatest poets and musicians of his time.
His temper and conversation must certainly have endeared him to
his acquaintance, and rendered them partial to his productions ;
and the praise of such writers as Milton and Waller is durable
fame. . . . But bad as the music of Lawes appears to us, it seems
to have been sincerely admired by his contemporaries, in general.
It is not meant to insinuate that it was pleasing to poets only,
but that it was more praised by them than any other music of
the same time." (*Ibid.* 3. 393-395). (See also the criticisms in
Hawkins 4. 56, Davey, p. 289, the *Oxford History of Music* pp. 202-210,
and Grove's *Dict.* s. v. *Lawes.* Keightley, *Life,* pp. 312-313, quotes
Prof. Edward Taylor in an enthusiastic defense of Lawes against
the attacks of Burney.)

A modern estimate of Henry Lawes' music would be forced to
admit its excellence. His songs are far in advance of his time, and
it would seem that the minds of the poets, carefully trained in
combining sense with rhythm, were the only ones to appreciate the
fact. Lawes cannot claim credit for inventing recitative. He
composed in a style usually called " aria parlante," in which he
made the prosody of his text his principal care. Dr. Burney's
criticism of *Sweet Echo* is quite just as regards the musical accentuation and certain intervals, but Lawes' work as a whole shows

a very consistent use of " just note and accent." His melodies are also interesting, and in the boldness of some of the intervals they are distinctly modern.

It will be noted that Milton emphasizes not only the well-ordered arrangement of Lawes' music, but its melodic effectiveness as well. His " song " is not only " well-measured," but " tuneful " ; and his air is " smooth." (Cf. " smooth-dittied song," in *C*. 85.)

He regards alike the sense of the words and the flow of the music, and is never guilty of " committing short and long."

APPENDIX III

I.

Ad Leonoram Romae canentem.

Angelus unicuique suus (sic credite, gentes)
Obtigit aethereis ales ab ordinibus.
Quid mirum, Leonora, tibi si gloria major ?
Nam tua praesentem vox sonat ipsa Deum.
Aut Deus, aut vacui certe mens tertia coeli,
Per tua secreto guttura serpit agens ;
Serpit agens, facilisque docet mortalia corda
Sensim immortali assuescere posse sono.
Quod, si cuncta quidem Deus est, per cunctaque fusus,
In te una loquitur, caetera mutus habet.

II.

Ad Eandem.

Altera Torquatum cepit Leonora poetam,
Cuius ab insano cessit amore furens.
Ah ! miser ille tuo quanto felicius aevo
Perditus, et propter te, Leonora, foret !
Et te Pieria sensisset voce canentem
Aurea maternae fila movere lyrae !
Quamvis Dircaeo torsisset lumina. Pentheo
Saevior, aut totus desipuisset iners,
Tu tamen errantes caeca vertigine sensus
Voce eadem poteras composuisse tua ;
Et poteras, aegro spirans sub corde quietem,
Flexanimo cantu restituisse sibi.

III.

Ad Eandem.

Credula quid liquidam Sirena, Neapoli, jactas,
Claraque Parthenopes fana Acheloiados ;
Littoreamque tua defunctam Naiada ripa,
Corpore Chalcidico sacra dedisse rogo ?
Illa quidem vivitque, et amoena Tibridis unda
Mutavit rauci murmura Pausilipi.
Illic, Romulidum studiis ornata secundis,
Atque homines cantu detinet atque deos.

It seems to have been the fashion to address epigrams to
Leonora.   A volume entitled *Applausi poetici alle glorie della
Signora Leonora Baroni* was published at Rome in 1639, containing Greek, Latin, Italian, French, and Spanish poems in
praise of the singer.[1]

Giovanni Battista Doni,[2] compares both her and her
mother with the poetess Sappho.[3]

Fulvio Testi wrote a sonnet in praise of her singing and
her beauty.[4]

An interesting eulogy of Leonora is to be found in a *Discours
sur la Musique d'Italie* by M. Mangars, Prior of S. Peter de
Mac, Paris, 1672 : " Leonora has fine parts, and a happy judgment in distinguishing good from bad music ; she understands
it perfectly well, and even composes, which makes her absolute mistress of what she sings, and gives her the most exact
pronunciation and expression of the sense of the words . . .
She sings with an air of confident and liberal modesty, and
with a pleasing gravity.   Her voice reaches a large compass of
notes, is just, clear, and melodious ; and she softens or raises
it without constraint or grimace.   Her raptures and sighs are
not too tender ; her looks have nothing impudent, nor do her

---

[1] See Nicias Erythreus, *Pinacotheca* 2. 427, Lips. 1712.

[2] Cf. p. 22.

[3] *De Praestantia Musicae Veteris*, 1647, 2. 56.   See Hawkins
4. 196.

[4] *Poesie del Conte Fulvio Testi*, Milano, 1658, p. 122.

gestures betray anything beyond the reserve of a modest girl. In passing from one song to another, she shows sometimes the divisions of the enharmonic and chromatic species with so much air and sweetness, that every hearer is ravished with that delicate and difficult mode of singing. She has no need of any person to assist her with a theorbo or viol, one of which is required to make her singing complete ; for she plays perfectly well herself on both those instruments. In short, I have been so fortunate as to hear her sing several times above thirty different airs, with second and third stanzas of her own composition. But I must not forget, that one day she did me the particular favor to sing with her mother and her sister ; her mother played upon the lute, her sister upon the harp, and herself upon the theorbo. This concert, composed of three fine voices, and of three different instruments, so powerfully captivated my senses, and threw me into such raptures, that I forgot my mortality, *et crus être déjà parmi des anges, jouissant des contentements des bienheureux.*" [1]

The mention of the mother's lute (*lyra*) in *Ep.* 2. 6, shows that Milton himself probably heard a concert of the kind described above. The line is a reminiscence of Buchanan's " Aureaque Orpheae fila fuisse lyrae," *El.* 7, noted by Todd, and also of Ovid's " fila dedisse lyrae," *Fast.* 5. 105.[2]

[1] See Bayle, *Dict.*, s. v. *Baroni*, quoted by Warton and Hawkins 4. 197. Cf. also Warton's note of the eulogy of Pietro della Velle, and Masson, *Life* 1. 751-753.

[2] See p. 32, and s. v. *lyra*, G.

APPENDIX IV

On the Music of the Spheres.

If there is any chance, fellow-students, for my slender abilities, after you have listened to so many and so great orators to-day, I also shall forthwith try to express, according to my small measure, my good will towards the solemn celebration of this day, and shall follow, at a distance, as it were, this day-long triumph of eloquence. While, therefore, I completely shun and dread those trite and commonplace subjects of discourse, the thought of this day and also of those who, as I rightly suspected, would speak worthily of the occasion, kindles and immediately arouses my mind to an arduous attempt with some other new material; and these two influences could indeed have stimulated even some sluggish person and have sharpened a mind otherwise obtuse. Therefore, it occurs to me to offer, with open hand, as they say, and abundance of oratory, at least a few prefatory words concerning that celestial concent about which there is soon to be a dispute with closed fist; but I shall keep track of the course of time, which at once urges and restrains me. Nevertheless, my hearers, I should wish you to accept these words as though they were said in sport. For what sane man would have thought that Pythagoras, that god among philosophers, to whose name all mortals of his age yielded the palm with the most sacred veneration—who, I say, would have thought that he would ever have produced publicly an opinion of so uncertain foundation? Surely, if ever he taught the harmony of the spheres, and the circling of the heavens to the charm of melody, he wished by this wisely to signify the most friendly relations of the orbs, and their uniform revolutions for ever according to the fixed law of fate. In this, to be sure, he has imitated both the poets and, what is almost the same, the divine oracles, by whom no sacred and hidden mystery is exhibited to the people unless enveloped in some veil and disguise.[1] This was done by that best interpreter of Mother Nature, Plato, when he told how certain Sirens sit upon the separate heavenly orbs, that by their honeyed song they may enchant both gods and men.[2] Further, this universal concord and lovely concent, which Pythagoras, in poetic fashion, expressed by harmony, Homer also hinted at very strongly in that golden chain of Jove suspended from Heaven. [3]

But Aristotle, the imitator and constant calumniator of Pythagoras and Plato, eager to pave his way to glory with the wrecked theories of men so great, imputed to Pythagoras this unheard symphony of the heavens, and music of the spheres.[4] But if either fate or chance had suffered, O father Pythagoras, that your soul in its flight should have passed into me, certainly you would not then lack one to defend you readily, however deep your disrepute and long its durance. And yet why should not the celestial bodies, in those perennial circuits, produce musical sounds ? Or does it not seem just to you, Aristotle ? Verily, I should scarcely believe that your intelligences could have endured that sedentary labor of rolling the heavens for so many ages, unless that ineffable melody of the stars had kept them from leaving their places, and persuaded them to stay by the charm of music. But suppose you take away from heaven those fair intelligences, then you both give up the ministering gods to drudgery, and condemn them to a treadmill. Nay, Atlas himself would long ago have withdrawn his shoulders, to the immediate ruin of the heavens, had not that sweet concent charmed him with the

---

[1] By this explanation of the Pythagorean theory Milton shows clearly his own interpretation of the mystical notion of a universal harmony. Cf. above, pp. 96-98.

[2] *Singulis coelis orbibus Sirenas quasdam insidere tradidit.* Milton adapts the words of Macrobius (*Comm. in Somn. Scip.* 2. 3) : ' singulas ait Sirenas singulis orbibus insidere,' referring to Plato, *Rep.* 10. 617.

[3] Cf. the description in *P. L.* 3. 570 ff.

[4] A reference to Aristotle's criticism of the Pythagorean system, *De Coelo* 2. 2-10.

greatest pleasure while panting and sweating under his burden.
Besides, the Dolphin, utterly disgusted at the stars, would
long ago have preferred the seas to heaven, had he not been
well aware that the vocal orbs of heaven far surpassed the
lyre of Arion in sweetness.[1]   What say you to the belief that
the very lark at day-break flies directly into the clouds, and
that the nightingale passes the whole solitude of night in song,
that they may order their melodies according to the harmonic
relations of heaven, to which they attentively listen ?   Thus
also the fable of the Muses dancing day and night around
about Jove's altars [2] has prevailed from the remotest beginning of things ; thus to Phoebus has been attributed from most
ancient times skill on the lyre.   Thus venerable antiquity
believed that Harmony was the daughter of Jove and Electra,
for when she was given to Cadmus in marriage, the whole
chorus of the heavens is said to have sounded in concord.[3]
But even supposing that no one on earth has ever heard this
symphony of the stars, shall all things above the sphere of
the moon be therefore mute, and sunk in drowsy stupor ?
Nay rather let us accuse our own feeble ears, which either
cannot, or deserve not to receive songs and sounds so sweet.
But this melody of the heavens is not wholly inaudible ; for
who would have thought, O Aristotle, of your goats capering
in mid-air,[4] unless because they clearly heard, by their
nearness, the heavens giving harmonious sounds, and were unable to restrain themselves from following the choirs ? But Pythagoras alone among mortals is said to have heard this con-

[1] Cf. Ovid, *Fast.* 2. 80 ff.

[2] Cf. *Il P.* 47-48 :

> And hears the Muses in a ring
> Aye round about Jove's altar sing.

[3] Harmonia was especially honored by the gods upon the occasion
of her marriage with Cadmus. Apollo, the Muses, and the Graces
are said to have sung and played, and she received gifts from all the
gods.   Milton alters the story so as to include the entire harmony
of heaven.   He probably derived his conception from Diodorus
5. 49. Cf. also Pind. *Pyth.* 3. 90 (160) ; Eurip. *Phoen.* 822.

[4] Cf. Aristotle, *Meteor.* 1. 4. 6 ; *Gen. An.* 4. 4. 15.

cent ; unless there had been someone, both a good genius and an inhabitant of heaven, who perchance by command of the gods came down to fill the minds of men with sacred learning, and to recall them to virtue ; at least he was certainly a man who contained all the numbers of virtues in himself, and who was worthy to mingle his words with those of the gods themselves, similar to his own, and to enjoy the consort of the celestials,[1] and therefore I do not wonder that the gods in very friendship permitted him to have a share [2] in the most hidden secrets of Nature.[3]   But that we should have very little perception of this harmony seems to have been caused by the audacity of the thievish Prometheus,[4] which brought so many evils upon men, and at the same time took away from us this happiness which we may never enjoy as long as we sink deeper and deeper into the violence and lusts of brutes.   For how can we be made capable of grasping this celestial sound when our minds, as Persius says,[5] are bent down towards the earth and completely empty of celestial things ?   But if we bore pure, chaste, snow-clean hearts, as once Pythagoras did, then

---

[1] Cf. " celestial consort," *S. M.* 27.

[2] *Abditissimis eum naturae secretis interesse permiserint.* Cf. Macrobius, *Comm. in Somn. Scip.* 2. 4. 15 : " Sed voluit intellegi, quod se eius qui caelestibus meruit interesse secretis completae aures sunt soni magnitudine, superest, ut ceterorum hominum sensus mundanae concinentiae non capiat auditum."

[3] Cf. above, p. 98. In this description of Pythagoras Milton may well have had in mind the character of Christ also.

[4] The myth of Prometheus and his theft of the divine fire corresponds here to the story of Adam's disobedience, when

> disproportioned Sin
> Jarred against Nature's chime, and with harsh din
> Broke the fair music that all creatures made. *S. M.* 19-21.

[5] *In terras curvae sunt, et coelestium prorsus inanes.* Persius (2. 61) reads, " O curvae in terris animae et caelestium inanis." Milton evidently took the reference from Lactantius, *Instit. Div.* ii. 2, where it is quoted " O curvae in terras animae et caelestium inanes." Lactantius interprets the line much as Milton does here, implying a difference between man and the quadrupeds.

indeed our ears should resound with that sweetest music of the circling stars and be filled with it. Then all things should return immediately as if to that golden age.[1] Then, free at last from our miseries, we should lead a life of ease, blessed and enviable even by the gods. Here, however, time cuts me off, as in the midst of my journey, and very opportunely, I suspect, for I should not with my irregular and unrhythmical style bawl aloud all this time, when I am proclaiming a harmony, and be myself the obstruction that prevents your hearing it. Therefore, I am done ! (Translation based in part upon Masson, *Life* 1. 279—281).

[1] Cf. *H.* 133-135.

> For if such holy song
> Enwrap our fancy long,
> Time will run back and fetch the Age of Gold.

APPENDIX V

A. Concerning Number, Motion, and Proportion.

Plato, *Republic* 7. 530–531 (tr. Jowett) :

"Motion, I said, has many forms, and not one only . . . It would seem, I said, that one is to the ears what the other is to the eyes ; for I conceive that as the eyes are appointed to look up at the stars, so are the ears to hear harmonious motions . . . There is a perfection which all knowledge ought to reach and which our pupils ought also to attain, and not to fall short of this, as I was saying that they did in astronomy. For in the science of harmony, as I dare say you know, they are equally empirical. The sounds and consonances which they compare are those which are heard only, and their labor, like that of the astronomers, is in vain. . . . I am speaking of the Pythagoreans, of whom I was just now proposing to inquire about harmony. For they too are in error, like the astronomers ; they investigate the numbers of the harmonies which are heard, but they never attain to problems—that is to say, they never reach the natural harmonies of number, or reflect why some numbers are harmonious and others not."

Plato, *Timaeus* 80 (tr. Jowett) :

"[The principle of universal motion explains] also the nature of sounds, whether swift or slow, sharp or flat, which are sometimes discordant on account of the inequality of the motion which they excite in us, and then again harmonical on account of their equality ; for the slower sounds reach the motions of the antecedent swifter sounds when these begin to pause and come to an equality, and after a while overtake and propel them. When they overtake them they do not introduce another or discordant motion, but they make the slower motion by degrees correspond with the swifter ; and when the motion leaves off, they assimilate them and cause a single mixed expression to be produced from sharp and flat, whence

arises a pleasure which even the unwise feel, and which to
the wise becomes a higher sort of delight, as being an imitation
of divine harmony in mortal motions."

See also *Timaeus* 35—40 ; 69 ; Aristotle, *Met.* 1. 5 ; Aristoxenus, *Harm.* 1. 8 ; 9 ; 10 ; 2. 32—34 ; Macrobius, 2. 2 ;
Boethius, *De Musica* 1 3 ; 16—19 ; 29—33 ; 2. 7—31 ; 3. 1—16 ;
4. 1—2 ; 4—13 ; Morley 202 ; Boeckh, *Kl. Schriften* 3. 169 ff.,
gives a detailed explanation of the Pythagorean system of
numbers.

Morley, p. 31 ; 242 :

Morley calls proportion " the comparing of numbers placed
perpendicularly one over another." In explanation of this he
continues, " Indeed we do not in music consider the numbers
by themselves, but set them for a sign to signify the altering of
our notes in the time." In his " annotations " to this passage
he enters upon a laborious discussion of the varieties and uses
of proportion. He explains that the term " proportion "
is really a misnomer, for it represents the *ratio et habitudo*
of numbers, for which there is no accurate translation in
English. He then describes arithmetical and geometrical
proportion and gives the following explanation of " harmonical proportion " :

" Harmonical proportion is that which neither is made of
equal habitudes, nor of the like differences ; but when the
greatest of three terms is so to the least as the difference of the
greatest and middle terms is to the difference of the middle
and least example. Here be three numbers, 6, 4, 3, where
the first two are in sesquialtera habitude, and the latter two
are in sesquitertia ; you see here is neither like habitude, nor
the same differences, for four is more than three by one, and
six is more than four by two ; but take the difference between
six and four, which is two, and the difference of 4 and 3, which
is 1, and compare the differences together, you shall find 2
to 1, as 6 is to 3, that is dupla habitude. And this is called
harmonical proportion, because it containeth the habitudes
of the consonants amongst themselves ; as, Let there be three
lines taken for as many strings or organ-pipes, let the first

be six foot long, the second four, the third three ; that of six will be a diapason or eighth to that of three, and that of four will be a diapente or fifth above that of six."

Morley, however, uses " proportion " only as applied to rhythm in music. He gives a " table containing all the usual proportions " (p. 38), but recommends only five of the simplest kind for common use—" Dupla, Tripla, Quadrupla, Sesquialtera, and Sesquitertia " (p. 31.)   See also Kircher, *Mus. Univ.* 2. 2 ; 3. 1.

B. *Concerning Harmony, Concord, and Discord.*

Plato, *Symposium* 187 (tr. Jowett) :

" Harmony is composed of differing notes of higher or lower pitch which disagreed once, but are now reconciled by the art of music ; for if the higher and lower notes still disagreed, there could be no harmony, as is indeed evident. For harmony is a symphony, and symphony is an agreement ; but an agreement of disagreements while they disagree cannot exist ; there is no harmony of discord and disagreement. This may be illustrated by rhythm, which is composed of elements short and long, once differing and now in accord ; which accordance, as in the former instance, medicine, so in this, music, implants, making love and unison to grow up among them ; and thus music, too, is concerned with the principles of love in their application to harmony and rhythm."

Plato, *Laws* 2. 665 (tr. Jowett) :

" Now the order of motion is called rhythm, and the order of the voice, in which high and low are duly mingled, is called harmony ; and both together are termed choric song."

Plato, *Phaedo* 86 (tr. Jowett) :

" Might not a person say . . . that harmony is a thing invisible, incorporeal, fair, divine, abiding in the lyre which is harmonized, but that the lyre and the strings are matter and material, composite, earthy, and akin to mortality ?   And when someone breaks the lyre, or cuts and rends the strings, then he who takes this view would argue . . . that the harmony survives and has not perished ; for you cannot imagine, as he would say, that the lyre without the strings, and the broken strings themselves remain, and yet that the harmony, which is of heavenly and immortal nature and kindred, has perished —and perished too before the mortal. That harmony, he would say, certainly exists somewhere, and the wood and strings will decay before that decays. For I suspect, Socrates, that the notion of the soul which we are all of us inclined to entertain, would also be yours, and that you too would conceive the body to be strung up, and held together, by the elements of hot and cold, wet and dry, and the likes, and that the soul is the harmony or due proportionate admixture of them."

Aristoxenus, *Harmonics* 20 (tr. Macran) :

" The nature of melody in the abstract determines which concord has the least compass. Though many smaller intervals than the Fourth occur in melody, they are without exception discords. But while the least concordant interval is thus determined, we find no similar determination for the greatest ; for as far at any rate as the nature of melody in the abstract is concerned, concords seem capable of infinite extension just as much as discords. If we add to an octave any concord, whether greater than, equal to, or less than, an octave, the sum is a concord. From this point of view, then, there is no maximum concord."

Aristotle, *Problems* 19. 38 (tr. Macran, *Notes to Aristoxenus*, p. 236) :

" The reason that we take pleasure in concord is that it is a blending of opposites that have a relation to one another. Now relation is order, and we saw that order naturally gave pleasure."

See also Aristotle, *Politics* 1. 5 ; Aristides, ed. Meibom, 12. 21 ; Bacchius, ed. Meibom, 2. 28 ; Gaudentius, ed. Meibom, 11. 17 ; Isagoge, ed. Meibom, 8. 24 ; Boethius, *De Musica* 1. 3 ; 5 ; 10 ; 5. 1—18 ; Morley, pp. 76—77 ; and Boeckh, *Kl. Schriften*, 3. 137.

C. Concerning the Modes, the Ethical Qualities of Music, and its Place in Education.

Plato, *Republic* 3. 398–399 (tr. Jowett) :

" 'And which are the harmonies expressive of sorrow? As you are a musician, I wish you would tell me.'

" 'The harmonies which you mean are the mixed or tenor Lydian, and the full-toned or bass Lydian, and others which are like them.' . . . .

" 'Which are the soft or drinking harmonies?' 'The Ionian,' he replied, 'and the Lydian; they are termed » solute.«'

" ' Well, and are these of any military use ? '

" ' Quite the reverse,' he replied ; ' but then the Dorian and the Phrygian appear to be the only ones which remain.'

" I answered : ' Of the harmonies I know nothing, but I want to have one warlike, which will sound the word or note which a brave man utters in the hour of danger and stern resolve, or when his cause is failing, and he is going to wounds or death or is overtaken by some other evil, and at every such crisis meets fortune with calmness and endurance.' "

Plato, *Laches* 188 (tr. Jowett) :

" When I hear a man discoursing of virtue, or of any sort of wisdom, who is a true man and worthy of his theme, I am delighted beyond measure ; and I compare the man and his words, and note the harmony and correspondence of them. And such a one I deem to be the true musician, having in himself a fairer harmony than that of the lyre, or any pleasant instrument of music ; for truly he has in his own life a harmony of words and deeds arranged, not in the Ionian, or in the Phrygian mode, nor yet in the Lydian, but in the true Hellenic mode, which is the Dorian, and no other."

Plato, *Protagoras* 326 (tr. Jowett) :

" The teachers of the lyre take . . . care that their young disciple is temperate and gets into no mischief ; and when they have taught him the use of the lyre, they introduce him to the poems of other excellent poets, who are the lyric poets ; and these they set to music, and make their harmonies and rhythms quite familiar to the children, in order that they

may learn to be more gentle, and harmonious, and rhythmical, and so more fitted for speech and action ; for the
life of man in every part has need of harmony and rhythm."

Cf. *Laws* 2. 654 ff.; 7. 802 ; 812.

Aristotle, *Politics* 8. 5. 1339 ; 1340 ; 1342 (tr. Jowett) :

" It is not easy to determine the nature of music, or why
any one should have a knowledge of it. Shall we say, for
the sake of amusement and relaxation, like sleep or drinking,
which are not good in themselves, but are pleasant, and at the
same time 'make care to cease,' as Euripides says ? And
therefore men rank them with music, and make use of all
three,—sleep, drinking, music,—to which some add dancing.
Or shall we agree that music conduces to virtue, on the ground
that it can form our minds and habituate us to true pleasures
as our bodies are made by gymnastic to be of a certain
character ? Or shall we say that it contributes to the enjoyment of leisure and mental cultivation, which is a third alter-
native ? . . . The first question is whether music is or is not to
be a part of education. Of the three things mentioned in
our discussion, which is it ?—Education or amusement or
intellectual enjoyment, for it may be reckoned under all three,
and seems to share in the nature of all of them. . . . In addition to this common pleasure, felt and shared in by all (for
the pleasure given by music is natural, and therefore adapted
to all ages and characters), may it not have also some influence
over the character and the soul ? It must have such an influence if characters are affected by it. And that they are
so affected is proved by the power which the songs of Olympus
and of many others exercise ; for beyond question they inspire enthusiasm, and enthusiasm is an emotion of the ethical
part of the soul. Besides, when men hear imitations, even
unaccompanied by melody or rhythm, their feelings move in
sympathy. . . . Rhythm and melody supply imitations of anger
and gentleness, and also of courage and temperance and of
virtues and vices in general, which hardly fall short of the
actual affections, as we know from our own experience, for in
listening to such strains our souls undergo a change. . . . Even
in mere melodies there is an imitation of character, for the

musical notes differ essentially from one another, and those who hear them are differently affected by each. Some of them make men sad and grave, like the so-called Mixolydian, others enfeeble the mind, like the relaxed harmonies, others, again, produce a moderate and settled temper, which appears to be the peculiar effect of the Dorian. . . . The whole subject has been well treated by philosophical writers on this branch of education, and they confirm their arguments by facts. The same principles apply to rhythms : some have a character of rest, others of motion, and of these latter again, some have a more vulgar, others a nobler movement. Enough has been said to show that music has a power of forming the character, and should therefore be introduced into the education of the young. . . . There seems to be in us a sort of affinity to harmonies and rhythms, which makes some philosophers say that the soul is a harmony, others, that she possesses harmony. . . . We accept the division of melodies proposed by certain philosophers into ethical melodies, melodies of action, and passionate or inspiring melodies, each having, as they say, a mode or harmony corresponding to it. But we maintain further that music should be studied, not for the sake of one, but of many benefits, that is to say with a view to education, purification, . . . for intellectual enjoyment, for relaxation and for recreation after exertion. . . . In education ethical melodies are to be preferred, but we may listen to the melodies of action and passion when they are performed by others. For feelings such as pity and fear, or, again, enthusiasm, exist very strongly in some souls, and have more or less influence over all. . . . For the purposes of education, as I have already said, those modes and melodies should be employed which are ethical, such as the Dorian ; though we may include any others which are approved by philosophers who have had a musical education. . . . All men agree that the Dorian music is the gravest and manliest and whereas we say that the extremes should be avoided, and the mean followed, and whereas the Dorian is between the other harmonies (the Phrygian and the Lydian), it is evident that our youth should be taught the Dorian music."

Kircher, *Mus. Univ.* 7. 5:

" Dores enim cum natura mites, et benevoli, in Deorum cultus singulari pietate ferrentur, melodiam inclinationi eorum convenientem, cuiusmodi Doria erat, colabant."

See also Aristotle, *Rep.* 4. 3 ; 8. 7 ; Plutarch, *De Musica* 13 ; 22 ; Aristoxenus 37 ff.; Boethius, *De Musica* 1. 1 ; 27 ; 4. 14—18 ; Macrobius, *Comm. in Somn. Scip.* 2. 3 ; 13—16 ; 4 ; Aristides 25 ; 1. 22 ; Ptolemaeus 2. 6 ; 10 ; and the references in Gevaert, *La Musique de l'Antiquité* 1. 178 ff.

D. *Concerning the Music of the Spheres.*

Plato, *Republic* 10. 617 (tr. Jowett) :

" The spindle turns on the knees of Necessity ; and on the upper surface of each circle is a siren, who goes round with them hymning a single sound and note. The eight together form one harmony, and round about, at equal intervals, there is another band, three in number, each sitting upon her throne ; these are the Fates, daughters of Necessity. . . . who accompany with their voices the harmony of the sirens."

Plato, *Iimaeus* 40 (tr. Jowett) :

"Vain would be the labor of telling about all the figures of them moving as in a dance, and their meetings with one another, and the return of their orbits on themselves, and their approximations, and to say which of them in their conjunctions meet and which of them are in opposition, and how they get behind and before one another, and at what times they are severally eclipsed to our sight and again reappear."

Cicero, in that fragment of his treatise *De Republica* called the *Somnium Scipionis* (6. 17, 18, tr. Edmonds), gives an elaborate account of the sphere-music. He describes the universe, with its nine circles or spheres, of which Heaven is the outermost, controlling the rest. The seven inner spheres, namely those of Saturn, Jupiter, Mars, the Sun, Venus, Mercury, and the Moon, " move in a contrary direction." The earth is immovable. " Which, as I was gazing at in amazement, I said as I recovered myself : ' From whence proceed these sounds so strong, and yet so sweet, that fill my ears ' ? ' The melody,' replies he, ' which you hear, and which, though composed in unequal time, is nevertheless divided into regular harmony, is effected by the impulse and motion of the spheres themselves, which, by a happy temper of sharp and grave notes, regularly produce various harmonic effects. Now it is impossible that such prodigious movements should pass in silence ; and nature teaches that the sounds which the spheres at one extremity utter must be sharp, and those on the other extremity must be grave ; on which account, that highest revolution of the star-studded heaven, whose motion is more rapid, is carried on with a sharp and quick sound ; whereas this of the moon, which is situated the lowest, and at the other extremity, moves with the gravest sound. For the earth, the ninth sphere, re-maining motionless, abides invariably in the innermost position, occupying the central spot in the universe.

Now these eight directions, two of which, Mercury and Venus, have the same powers, effect seven sounds, differing in their modulations, which number is the connecting prin-ciple of almost all things. Some learned men, by imitating this harmony with strings and vocal melodies, have opened a way for their return to this place ; as all others have done, who, endued with pre-eminent qualities, have cultivated in their mortal life the pursuits of heaven. The ears of mankind, filled with these sounds, had become deaf, for of all your senses it is the most blunted . . . the sound, which is effected by the rapid rotation of the whole system of nature, is so powerful, that human hearing cannot comprehend it, just as you cannot look directly upon the sun, because your sight and sense are overcome by his beams.' " Cf. the elaborate comment of Macrobius, 2. 1—4 (quoted in part on p.150 below).

Pliny, *Nat. Hist.* 2. 3 (tr. Bostock and Riley, ed. Bohn) : " The rising and the setting of the sun clearly prove that this globe is carried round in the space of twenty-four hours, in an eternal and never-ceasing circuit, and with incredible swift-ness. I am not able to say, whether the sound caused by the whirling about of so great a mass be excessive, and, therefore, far beyond what our own ears can perceive, nor, indeed, whether the resounding of so many stars, all carried along at the same time and revolving in their orbits, may not produce a kind of delightful harmony of incredible sweetness. To us, who are in the interior, the world appears to glide silently along, both by day and by night."

Martianus Capella, *De Nupt. Phil.* 1. 27–28 :

" Superi autem globi orbesque septemplices suavis cuiusdam melodiae harmonicis tinnitibus concinabant ac sono ultra solitum dulciore, quippe Musas adventare praesenserant. Quae quidem singillatim circulis quibusque metatis ubi suae pulsum modulationis agnoverant, constiterunt. Nam Urania stellantis mundi sphaeram extimam continatur, quae acuto raptabatur sonora tinnitu. Polymnia Saturnium circulum tenuit, Euterpe Iovialem, Erato ingresse modulatur, Melpomene medium ubi Sol flammanti mundum lumine convenustat. Terpsichore Venerio sociatur auro. Calliope orbem complexa Cyllenium, Clio citimum circulum, hoc est in luna collocavit hospitium. Quae quidem gravis pulsus modis raucioribus personabat. Sola vero, quod vector eius cygnus impatiens oneris atque etiam subvolandi alumna stagna patierat, Thalia derelicta in ipso florentis campi ubere residebat."

Philo Judaeus, *De Somniis* 1. 6 ; 7 (tr. Yonge, ed. Bohn) :

"For these two things, the heaven and the mind, are the things which are able to utter, with all becoming dignity, the praises, and hymns, and glory, and beatitude of the father who created them : for man has received an especial honor beyond all other animals, namely, that of ministering to the living God. And the heaven is always singing melodies, perfecting an all-musical harmony, in accordance with the motions of all the bodies which exist therein ; of which, if the sound ever reached our ears, love, which could not be restrained, and frantic desires, and furious impetuosity, which could not be put an end to or pacified, would be engendered, and would compel us to give up even what is necessary, nourishing ourselves no longer like ordinary mortals on the meat and drink, which is received by means of our throat, but on the inspired songs of music in its highest perfection, as persons about to be made immortal through the medium of their ears ; and it is said that Moses was an incorporeal hearer of these melodies, when he went for forty days, and an equal number of nights, without at all touching any bread or any water.

Therefore the heaven, which is the archetypal organ of music, appears to have been arranged in a most perfect manner, for no other object except that the hymns, sung to the honour of the Father of the universe, might be attuned in a musical manner."

Isidorus, *Etymologiae* 3. 17 (Migne, *Patrologia Latina* 82. 163) :

"Nam et ipse mundus quadam harmonia sonorum fertur esse compositus, et coelum ipsum sub harmoniae modulatione revolvitur."

Ambrosius, *Enarrationes in XII Psalmos Davidicos, Prae-fatio,* 2. (Migne, *Patrologia Latina* 14. 1. 1) :

" Laudant angeli Dominum, psallunt ei potestates coelorum, et ante ipsum initium mundi Cherubim et Seraphim, cum suavitate canorae vocis suae dicunt, ' Sanctus, sanctus, sanctus *(Isa.* 6. 3).' Innumera angelorum milia assistunt et seniores et turba magna sicut voces aquarum multarum concinunt *Alleluia (Apoc.* 19. 1. 4. 6). Ipsum axem coeli fert expressior sermo cum quadam perpetui concentus suavitate versari, ut sonus eius extremis terrarum partibus audiretur, ubi sunt quaedam secreta naturae. . . . In scopulis quoque ipsis et lapidibus reperit natura quod delectaret. Alio-rum specula, aliorum usus delectat aut gratia. Ferae ipsae, at-que aves loci amoenioris aut modulatioris vocis delectatione mulcentur. Lactentibus quoque parvulis aut severitas terrori est, aut blanditiae voluptati. Naturalis igitur delectatio est."

Morley, pp. 228—229 :

Morley gives a table showing how the Greeks made a " comparison of the Times, Keys, Muses, and Planets." In another table, taken from " an old treatise of music written in vellum above an hundred years ago, called *Regulae Franconis cum additionibus Roberti de Haulo*," each of the planets is supplied with a definite note. In this scale, *Coelum* is represented as sounding an exact octave above *Terra,* " and at the end thereof, these words *Marcus Tullius*, pointing, as I take it, to that most excellent discourse in the dream of *Scipio*, where the motions and sounds of all the spheres are most sweetly set **down**; there *Tully* doth affirm that it is impossible that so great motions may be moved without sound; and according to their nearness to the earth, giveth he every one a sound, the lower body the lower sound.   But *Glareanus*, one of the most learned of our time, maketh two arguments to contrary effects, gathered out of their opinion, who deny the sound of the spheres.   The greatest bodies, saith he, make the greatest sounds.   The higher celestial bodies are the greatest bodies; therefore the highest bodies make the greatest sounds. The other proveth the contrary thus : That which moveth swiftest giveth the highest sound; the higher bodies move the swiftest; therefore the highest bodies give the highest sound."

See also Aristotle, *De Coelo* 2. 9 ; *Met.* 1, 5 ; 11. 8 ; 12. 8 ; Porphyr. *in Ptol. Harm.* 4, p. 251 ; Cicero, *De Nat. Deor.* 3. 11 ; Pliny, *Nat. Hist.* 2. 22. 20 ; Plutarch, *De Musica* 44 ; *Symp.* 9 ; Nicomachus, *Enchirid. Harm.* 1. 6, ed. Meibom, p. 33 ; Boethius, *De Musica* 1. 2 (quoted below, p. 149); 27; Isidorus, *De Nat. Rer.* 2 ; 12 ; 13 ; 22 ; 23 ; Kircher, *Mus. Univ.* 10. 1 ; and the references given by Gevaert, *La Musique de l'Antiquité* 1. 178 ff.

Cf. Hawkins 4. 158—166, describing Kepler's *Harmonices Mundi* ; Mersennus, *Harmonie Universelle* ; Hawkins 4. 168—173, describing the system of Robert Flud, and reproducing his diagram.

Cf. also the references to the sphere-myth in literature, given by Albert S. Cook, *Notes on Milton's Nativity Ode, Trans. Conn. Acad.* 15. 343—344.

E. *Concerning the Celestial and Mundane Music.*

Proclus, *On the Theology of Plato* 5. 35 :

" Quod enim est expers formae, et quod est infinitum, et quod est expers rhytmi, est materiae proprietas.   Quod igitur est immateriatum, et finitum, et impollutum, est rhytmo

praeditum, concinnum, et ordinatum, et intellectuale.   Prop-
terea enim et ipsum Coelum perpetuo choreas agitare dicitur,
et omnes in Coeli circuli motionem rhytmo praeditam, con-
cinnam, et harmonicam participant, quod superne ab impollu-
tis Diis facultate repleantur.   Quoniam enim circuli coelestes
in orbem moventur, ipsam Mentem effingunt, et intellectuale
circumvectionem exprimunt."

Boethius, *De Musica* 1. 2 :

" There are three kinds of Music : and the first is the Music of
the Universe (Musica Mundana), the second the Human
Music, the third that which is practiced on certain instruments,
e. g., the cithara, or the tibia, in short on all instruments on
which one can play a melody.   Now in the first place, one
can best recognize the Music of the Universe in those things
which one perceives in the heavens themselves, or in the combination of elements, or in the change of seasons.   How could
it happen otherwise, that the machinery of heaven should
be moved so quickly and in such a silent course ?   Although
that tone does not reach our ears—and that it should happen
in this wise is necessary for many reasons—still such an infinitely rapid motion of such great bodies cannot but bring forth
tones, especially as the courses of the planets are connected
by so great a Harmony that nothing more thoroughly ordered
and adjusted is known.'

Macrobius, *Comm. in Somn. Scip.* 1. 6. 42—43 :

"Ternarius vero adsignat animam tribus suis partibus ab-
solutam, quarum prima est ratio, quam λογιστικόν appellant,
secunda animositas, quam θυμικόν vocant, tertia cupiditas,
quae ἐπιθυμιστικόν nuncupatur.   Item nullus sapientum
animam ex symphoniis quoque musicis constitisse dubitavit.
Inter has non parvae potentiae est, quae dicitur διὰ πασῶν."

See also Martianus Capella, *De Nupt. Phil.* 1. 27—28 ;
Pseud. Dionysius, *De Coelesti Hier.* cap. 10 ; Isidorus, *Etym.*
3. 16 ; *De Nat. Rer.* 12 ; Anselm, *De Imagine Mundi* 1 ;
Kircher, *Mus. Univ.* 10. 1. 2.

F. Concerning the Significance of Music.

Plutarch, *De Musica* 23 :

"But the most important thing, my friends, which music in its highest significance reveals, you have still overlooked. The rotation of the universe and the motion of the planets could neither begin nor continue without music, according to Pythagoras, Archytas, Plato and the other ancient philosophers. For everything, they say, is ordered by God according to the laws of Harmony."

Macrobius, *Comm. in Somn. Scip.* 2. 3. 7—12 :

"Nam ideo in hac vita omnis anima musicis sonis capitur, ut non soli qui sunt habitu cultiores verum universae quoque barbarae nationes cantus quibus vel ad ardorem virtutis animentur vel ad mollitiem voluptatis resolvantur exerceant, quia in corpus defert memoriam musicae cuius in caelo fuit conscia, et ita delenimentis canticis occupatur, ut nullum sit tam inmite tam asperum pectus, quod non oblectamentorum talium teneatur affectu.   Hinc aestimo et Orphei vel Amphionis fabulam, quorum alter animalia ratione carentia alter saxa quoque trahere cantibus ferebantur, sumpsisse principium, quia primi forte gentes vel sine rationis cultu barbaras vel saxi instar nullo affectu molles ad sensum voluptatis canendo traxerunt. Ita denique omnis habitus animae cantibus gubernatur, ut et ad bellum progressui et item receptui canatur cantu et excitante et rursus sedante virtutem : *dat somnos adimitque*,[1] nec non curas et inmittit et retrahit, iram suggerit, clementiam suadet, corporum quoque morbis medetur ; nam hinc est quod aegris remedia praestantes praecinere dicuntur.   Et quid mirum, si inter homines musicae tanta dominatio est, cum aves quoque, ut lusciniae, ut cygni aliaeve id genus, cantum veluti quadam disciplina artis exerceant, nonnullae vero vel aves vel terrenae seu aquatiles beluae, invitante cantu in retia sponte decurrant, et pastoralis fistula pastum progressis quietem imperet gregibus ? Nec mirum.   Inesse enim mundanae animae causas musicae,

---

[1] Virg. *Aen.* 4. 244.

quibus est intexta, praediximus ; ipsa autem mundi anima viventibus omnibus vitam ministrat :

Hinc hominum pecudumque genus vitaeque volantum
Et quae marmoreo fert monstra sub aequore pontus.[1]

Iure igitur musica capitur omne quod vivit, quia caelestis anima, qua animatur universitas, originem sumpsit ex musica. Haec, dum ad sphaeralem motum mundi corpus inpellit, sonum efficit qui *intervallis* est *disiunctus inparibus, sed tamen pro rata parte ratione distinctis,* sicut a principio ipsa contexta est."

Kircher, *Mus. Univ.* 2. 3 :

"Solus itaque perfectus Musicus est, et dici debet, qui Theoriam praxi iungit, qui non tantum componere novit, sed et singularum rerum rationem reddere potest ; ad quod tamen cum dignitate praestandum, omnium paene scientiarum notitia requiritur ; scilicet Arithemeticae, Geometriae, Proportionum sonorum, Musicae practicae tam vocalis, quam instrumentalis, Metricae, Historicae, Dialecticae, Rhetoricae, totius denique Philosophiae absoluta cognitio, adeo ut Musicam in rigore sumptam, nihil aliud esse definiamus, quam *Sonorum harmonicorum, in quocumque genere occurentium perfectam scientiam.*"

See also Plato, *Tim.* 47 ; 80 (quoted above, p. 137) ; *Phaedrus* 245 ; 265 ; Aristotle, *Politics* 1. 5 ; Kircher, *Mus. Univ.* 2. 6. 2 ; 7. 1. 1 ; 9. 3 ; 10. 4 ; 9 ; 10.

---

[1] Lactantius, *De falsa Rel.* 1. 5.

The Glossary has been prepared with a three-fold purpose, (1) to show the extent and the variety of Milton's vocabulary in musical terms, (2) to show his frequent special musical use of terms of larger general meaning, and (3) to give an exact meaning of many such terms in the light of his peculiar use of them, and of his highly specialized knowledge of music. The words in the Glossary are taken not only from the English Poems, but from the Latin and Italian Poems and the Prose Works as well. Wherever a definition is obvious it has been omitted.

ABBREVIATIONS OF TITLES.

A. = *Arcades.*
C. = *Comus.*
Circ. = *Upon the Circumcision.*
De Sphaer. Con. = *De Sphaerarum Concentu.*
H. = *Hymn on the Nativity.*
Hist. Brit. = Lines from the *History of Britain.*
Il P. = *Il Penseroso.*
It. S. = *Italian Sonnet.* (The Italian Sonnets are numbered as in Pattison's edition.)
L. = *Lycidas.*
L'A. = *L'Allegro.*
M. M. = *Song on a May Morning.*
M. W. = *Epitaph on the Marchioness of Winchester.*
P. = *The Passion.*
P. L. = *Paradise Lost.*
P. R. = *Paradise Regained.*
Ps. = Translations of the Psalms.
P. W. = *Prose Works* (Bohn Edition).
S. = *Sonnet.* (The English Sonnets are numbered as in Bradshaw's *Concordance.*)
S. A. = *Samson Agonistes.*
S. M. = *At a Solemn Music.*
T. = *On Time.*
U. C. = *On the University Carrier* (two poems).
V. Ex. = *At a Vacation Exercise.*

LATIN POEMS:

Ad Leon. = *Ad Leonoram.*

Ad Mans. = *Ad Mansum.*

Ad P. = *Ad Patrem.*

Ad Rous. = *Ad Rousium.*

Ad Sals. = *Ad Salsillum.*

De Id. Plat. = *De Idea Platonica Quemadmodum Aristoteles Intellexit.*

E. = *Elegia.*

Ep. = *Epigram.*

Epit. Dam. = *Epitaphium Damonis.*

In Quint. Nov. = *In Quintum Novembris.*

In Obit. Praes. Eli. = *In Obitum Praesulis Eliensis.*

Nat. non pat. sen. = *Naturam non Pati Senium.*

GLOSSARY

Aeolian, adj. *Pertaining to the Aeolian mode in music, or to the Aeolian style of poetry* : *P. R.* 4. 257.

Air, n. 1. *A musical composition for a single voice, or for voices in unison, with instrumental accompaniment, and without counterpoint* : *S.* 20. 12 ; *P. W.* 2. 73.
> 2. *A melody* : *P. R.* 2. 362 ; *P.* 27 ; *L'A.* 136 ; *S.* 8. 12 ; *S.* 13. 8.

Alchymy, n. *A mixed metal, resembling gold, with brass as the chief constituent,* used for making trumpets. As the trumpet itself : *P. L.* 2. 517. Cf. *metal.*

Alternare, L. v. intr. *Sing or dance by turns* : *Ad. Sals.* 5.

Alternate, v. tr. *Sing by turns.* Possibly with a suggestion of dancing : *P. L.* 5. 657. Cf. *Ad Sals.* 5.

Angel-trumpets, n. pl. : *S. M.* 11. See *trumpet.*

Anthem, n. *A composition for voices, with or without accompaniment, used in divine service* : *P. R.* 4. 594 ; *H.* 219 ; *Il P.* 163.

Antimasque, n. *A grotesque interlude between the acts of a masque* : *P. W.* 1. 450.

Antiphony, n. *A response in sacred music* : *P. W.* 2. 61.

Apollo, n. As the god of music : *V. Ex.* 37 ; *C.* 478 ; *P. W.* 3. 488 ; *E.* 6. 34 ; *Ad Mans.* 57 ; *Ad Rous.* 35. See also *Delius, Paean, Phoebus.*

Arion, n. *A mythical Greek musician* : *Ad P.* 60 ; *De Sphaer. Con.,* App. IV. p. 134, l. 5.

Arundo, L. n. *Shepherd's-pipe* : *E.* 5. 113. See *cicuta, oat, pipe, reed.*

Attic bird : *P. R.* 4. 245. See *nightingale.*

Auditory, n. *An audience listening to music* : *P. W.* 3. 62 ; 152.

Bacchus, L. n. Represented as having an interest in music : *E.* 6. 14 ; 23 ; 34 ; *Ad Sals.* 28. Cf. *Epit. Dam.* 219.

Bag-pipe, n. Used as a *rustic instrument* : *P. W.* 2. 73.

Ballad, n. *Folk-song* : *P. W.* 2. 57.

Ballad-singer, n. : *P. W.* 1. 25 ; 138.

Ballatry, n. *Ballad tunes without their words* : *P. W.* 2. 73.

Barbitos, Gr. n. *An ancient lyre.* Its sides were long and narrow, and it had very long strings. Used by the Lesbians and Anacreon, primarily for songs of joy: *E.* 6. 37; *Ad Rous.* 9. See *lyre.*

Bard, n. 1. *Minstrel* : *P. L.* 7. 34 ; *L.* 53 ; *P. W.* 3. 491.

2. *Poet as singer* : *Il P.* 116 ; *C.* 45 ; *P. W.* 1. 236.

Cf. *E.* 1. 21 ; 6. 77 ; *De Id. Plat.* 28 ; *Ad P.* 85 ; *S.* 13. 10 ; and see *Demodocus, Druids.*

Bass, n. *The fundamental part in musical harmony* : *H.* 130.

Bell, n. As producing musical tone : *L'A.* 93 ; *P. W.* 3. 112.

Blast, n. 1. *Current of air producing sound in an organ* : *P. L.* 1. 708.

2. *Blowing of a trumpet* : *S. A.* 972.

3. *Sound of a trumpet* : *P. L.* 11. 76 ; *H.* 161 ; *P. W.* 1. 232.

Blow, v. 1. tr. *Produce sounds upon wind-instruments* : *P. L.* 1. 540 ; 11. 73 ; *S. M.* 11.

2. *Announce by a trumpet-blast* : *Ps.* 81. 9.

3. intr. *Give forth sounds*, of wind-instruments : *P. L.* 6. 60 ; *H.* 130 ; *Il P.* 161.

4. Fig., of winds, with musical significance : tr. *P. L.* 2. 717; intr. *P. L.* 5. 192.

Bout, n. *A turn or involution in music* : *L'A.* 139.

Bray, v. tr. *Sound harshly* : *P. L.* 6. 209.

Brazen, adj. *Having the harsh sound of brass instruments* : *P. L.* 11. 713. Cf. aerisonam . . . tubam : *E.* 4. 80. See' *alchymy.*

Breathe, v. 1. tr. *Produce musical sounds by breathing* : *C.* 245 ; *H.* 179 ; cf. *P. R.* 4. 258.

2. Fig. of winds, with musical significance : *P. L.* 5. 193.

3. intr. *Give forth gentle sounds as of the voice or of wind-instruments* : *P. L.* 1. 709 ; *Il P.* 151. See *solemn-breathing.*

Buccina, L. n. Latin equivalent of *clarion* (q. v.) : *E.* 4. 118. See *trumpet.*

Cadence, n. *Melody gradually diminishing.* Fig. of music of the winds : *P. L.* 2. 287.

Camoena, L. n. *A type of water-nymphs associated with music,* usually identified with the Muses. Milton seems to have recognized a possible etymological connection with *carmen* or *canere* (cf. Macrobius, *Comm. in Somn. Scip.* 2. 3. 4) : *E.* 6. 3 ; *Ad P.* 67 ; *Ad Mans.* 5 ; *Epit. Dam.* 170 ; *Ad Sals.* 7. See *Musa.*

Canere, L. v. *Sing.* 1. tr. : *E.* 5. 28 ; 6. 28 ; 81 ; *Ad P.* 46 ; *Ad. Mans.* 11 ; 43 ; *Epit. Dam.* 73. See *sing,* I (3).

2. intr. : *Ad Leon.* 2. 5 ; *In Quint. Nov.* 62 ; *Ad P.* 54 ; *Epit. Dam.* 143. See *sing,* II.

Canorus, L. adj. *Melodious* : *Ad P.* 59 ; *Epit. Dam.* 34.

Cantare, L. v. *Sing.* 1. tr. : *In Quint. Nov.* 65 ; *P. W.* 1. 169. Cf. decantatum : *Ad P.* 119. See *sing,* I (3).

2. intr. : *E.* 6. 22. See *sing,* II.

Canting, v. adj. Possibly with connotation of *chanting* : *P. W.* 3. 152.

Cantus, L. n. *Song.* Especially of the melody : *E.* 5. 115 ; *Ad Leon.* 2. 12 ; 3. 8 ; *Ad P.* 52 ; *Ad Sals.* 32 ; *Ad Mans.* 44 ; *Epit. Dam.* 218. See *song* (3).

Carmen, L. n. *Song.* Especially of the words : *E.* 5. 5 ; 114 ; 6. 5 ; 6 ; 14 ; 34 ; *Ad P.* 21 ; 24 ; 26 ; 33 ; 37 ; 41 ; 54 ; 55 ; 115 ; *Ad Mans.* 1 ; 12 ; 46 ; 69 ; 80 ; *Epit. Dam.* 3. See *song* (2).

Carol, 1. v. tr. *Sing with joy* : *C.* 849.

    2. n. *Joyful song* : *P. L.* 12. 367.

Cetra, It. n. *A lyre.* Lat. *cithara* : *It. S.* 7. 12. See *cithara, lyre.*

Chains, n. pl. Fig. of the melodies involved in counterpoint : *L'A.* 143.

Chant, 1. v. tr. *Sing or intone solemnly* : *P. W.* 1. 466.

    2. n. *Song* : *P. R.* 2. 290.

Chanters, n. pl. *Choristers* : *P. W.* 2. 426.

Charm, 1. v. tr. *Conjure by song* : *P. L.* 1. 561 ; 787 ; 11. 132.

    2. n. *Song of birds* : *P. L.* 4. 642 ; 651.

    3. n. *Song.* Suggested by Lat. *carmen* : *P. L.* 2. 666 ; *P. R.* 4. 257 ; *Il P.* 83.

Charming, v. adj. 1. *Having the qualities of song, musical* : *P. L.* 3. 368 ; 5. 626 ; 8. 2 ; 11. 595 ; *C.* 476 ; *P. W.* 3. 476. Cf. *enchanting.*

    2. *Producing music with magical effect* : *P. W.* 3. 184. See *charm* (1).

Chelys, Gr. n. *The primitive, small-sized lyre.* To Milton, the classic equivalent of the lute : *E.* 6. 39. See *lyra, lyre.*

Chime, n. *Musical concord of sounds produced usually by vibration of metal surface or strings* : *P. L.* 11. 559 ; *H.* 128 ; *C.* 1021 ; *S. M.* 20.

Chiming, v. adj. *Sounding in concord, as in a chime* (q. v.) : *P. R.* 2. 363.

Choir, n. 1. *A band of singers.*

        a. In the church service : *Il P.* 162.

        b. In pagan worship : *Hist. Brit.* 6.

        c. At a wedding : *M. W.* 17.

        d. Of the angels : *P. L.* 4. 711 ; 7. 254 ; 12. 366 ; *P. R.* 1. 242 ; 4. 593 ; *H.* 27 ; 115 ; *S. M.* 12. Cf. *E.* 3. 59 ; 65 ; 5. 85 ; *Epit. Dam.* 218.

        e. Fig., of animals : *P. L.* 9. 198.

        f. Of birds : *P. L.* 4. 264.

g. Of the stars : *C.* 112. Cf. *Ad P.* 36.

h. Of the Muses : *S.* 13. 10. Cf. *Ad Mans.* 2.

2. *A company.* Of the angels, probably with musical significance : *P. L.* 3. 217 ; 666 ; 5. 251. See *choral, chorea, chorus.*

Choral, adj. a. *Singing parts in harmony* : *P. L.* 7. 599.

b. *Sung in chorus* : *P. L.* 5. 162.

Chord, n. 1. *A harp-string* : *P. L.* 11. 561. See *string.*

2. *A simultaneous combination of musical tones* : *P. W.* 3. 62 ; 476. Possibly also *P. L.* 11. 561.

Chorea, L. n. *A choral dance* : *E.* 6. 44 ; *Ad P.* 36.

Chorus, n. 1. *Song performed by a band of singers.*

a. Of angels : *P. L.* 7. 275.

b. Of the chorus in Greek tragedy : *P. R.* 4. 262.

2. *The band of singers performing the choruses in the classic drama* : *P. W.* 1. 244 ; 2. 479 (two reff.).

Chorus, L. n. 1. *A choir* (q. v.).

a. Of Satyrs : *E.* 5. 120 ; *Ad P.* 52.

b. Of Bacchic revellers : *E.* 6. 18 ; *Epit. Dam.* 218.

c. Of pagan worshippers : *De Id. Plat.* 28.

d. Of the Muses : *Ad Mans.* 2.

Chromatic, adj. *Having the characteristics of the chromatic genus in Greek music* : *S. M.* 19 (*variant*).

Cicuta, L. n. *Hemlock-reed, used as flute* : *E.* 6. 89 ; *Epit. Dam.* 135.

Cithara, Gr. n. *An ancient lyre.* The largest and most highly developed of the family, characterized by its large wooden sound-board and its broad hollow side-pieces : *Ad P.* 54 ; *Ad Mans.* 63 ; *Epit. Dam.* 89. See *cetra, lyre.*

Clamor, 1. v. tr. *Salute noisily* : *S. A.* 1621.

2. n. *Loud sound, noise.*

a. Of voices : *P. L.* 2. 862 ; 7. 36 ; *P. R.* 2. 148.

b. Of metal : *P. L.* 6. 208.

Clamorous, adj. *Noisy, discordant* : *P. L.* 10. 479 ; *S. M.* 20 (*variant*).

Clang, n. 1. *The sound of a trumpet* : *H.* 157.

2. *The noise of birds* : *P. L.* 7. 422 ; 11. 835.

Clarion, n. *A small, shrill trumpet* : *P. L.* 1. 532 ; fig., *P. L.* 7. 443. See *buccina, trumpet.*

Clash, v. 1. tr. *Strike with a confused, loud, metallic sound* : *P. L.* 1. 668.

2. intr. : *P. L.* 6. 209.

Clio, L. n. *The Muse of heroic poetry* : *Ad Mans.* 24 ; *E.* 4. 31.

Close, n. *The conclusion of a musical phrase* : *H.* 100 ; *C.* 548.

Composer, n. Of music : *P. W.* 3. 476.

Concent, n. *Musical concord.* Lat. *concentus* (q. v.) ; It. *concento,* the sounding of all the notes in a chord together—the opposite of *arpeggio* : *S. M.* 6.   Cf. *consent* : *Il P.* 95 ; *P. W.* 3. 67.

Concentus, L. n. *Musical concord* : *De Sphaer. Con., title* ; App. IV. p. 132, l. 16 ; 133. 28 ; 135. 1 ; *Mane citum lectus fuge, Comm. Bk.* p. 61.   See *concent.*

Concha, L. n. *The shell of Triton* : *Nat. non pat. sen.* 57.

Consonant, adj. *In concord* : *P. W.* 1. 161 ; 176.

Consort, n. 1. *A company of musicians* : *S. M.* 27.
    2. *Harmony* : *H.* 132 ; *Il P.* 145.   Possibly, *S. M.* 27.

Consortium, L. n. *Company, society.* With probable musical significance : *De Sphaer. Con.* App. IV, p. 135. 7.   See *consort.*

Counterpoint, n. *Melody added as an accompaniment to a given melody* : *C.* 243 *(variant).*

Cymbal, n. *H.* 208 ; *P. W.* 1. 377 ; 3. 366.

Dance, 1. v. tr. *Move rhythmically to the accompaniment of music.* Of the planets and spheres : *P. L.* 8. 125 ; 9. 103.
    2. intr. a. *Move with dignity and rhythm* : *P. L.* 6. 615 ; *Ps.* 87. 25.
        b. Of the planets and stars : *P. L.* 7. 374 ; *M. M.* 2.
        c. Fig., expressing joy : *P. L.* 5. 395.
    3. *Move with rhythmic grace, expressive of merriment.*
        a. Of fairies : *V. Ex.* 60.
        b. In rustic and pastoral surroundings : *L'A.* 96 ; *A.* 96 ; *C.* 883 ; *L.* 34.
    4. *Move in riotous carousal.*
        a. Connoting sensuality : *P. L.* 11. 619.
        b. Of witches : *P. L.* 2. 664.
    5. Fig. of a drug, *bubble merrily* : *C.* 673.   Cf. *dancing.*
    6. n. a. *Dignified, rhythmical motion, to the accompaniment of music* : *P. L.* 6. 615 ; 7. 324 ; *C.* 974.
        b. Expressive of joy : *P. L.* 4. 267.
        c. Of the angels : *P. L.* 5. 619 ; 620 ; 630.
        d. Of the planets : *P. L.* 3. 580 ; 5. 178.
        e. Of pagan rites : *H.* 210.
    7. *Dainty, graceful motion, expressive of merriment.*
        a. Of fairies : *P. L.* 1. 786.
        b. In rustic surroundings : *C.* 952.
    8. *Carousal, with musical accompaniment* : *P. L.* 4. 768 ; 11. 584 ; *C.* 104 ; 176.

9. *The music of a dance* : P. L. 8. 243. Cf. *E.* 5. 120 ; 6. 40-48 ; *Ad Sals.* 5 ; *Epit. Dam.* 85 ; 218-219 ; *Ad Rous.* 8.

Dancer, n. *S. A.* 1325 ; *P. W.* 2. 73.

Dancing, v. adj. a. Fig., of wine, *bubbling merrily* : *S. A.* 543. Cf. *dance* (5) above.

b. Contemptuously, of the clergy : *P. W.* 2. 6.

Delius, Lat. n. *Apollo as god of music* : *E.* 5. 13 ; 14. See *Apollo, Paean, Phoebus.*

Demodocus, n. *The minstrel of the Phaeacians* : *V. Ex.* 48.

Descant, 1. v. intr. *Improvise variations upon a set theme* : Fig., *S. A.* 1228.

2. n. *Extempore variations on a plain-song, or set theme* : *P. L.* 4. 603 ; *P. W.* 3. 476.

Diapason, n. *The interval of the octave.* " In perfect Diapason," *in parallel movement an octave lower* : *S. M.* 23.

Din, n. 1. *Loud, confused noise* : *P. L.* 1. 668 ; 2. 1040 ; 6. 408 ; 10. 521 ; 12. 61.

2. *Noise,* of the crowing of a cock : *L'A.* 49.

3. *Discord* : *S. M.* 20.

Discord, n. a. *Lack of concord* : *P. L.* 6. 210 ; 897 ; 7. 217 ; 9. 1124 ; *P. W.* 2. 33.

b. Personified : *P. L.* 2. 967 ; 10. 707 ; *In Quint. Nov.* 142.

Disproportion, n. *Discord* : Fig., *P. W.* 3. 392. See *disproportioned, proportion, well-proportioned.*

Disproportioned, v. adj. *Lacking in harmony* : *S. M.* 19. See *disproportion, proportion, well-proportioned.*

Dissonance, n. *Discord* : *P. L.* 7. 32 ; *C.* 550.

Dissonant, adj. *Discordant* : *S. A.* 662 ; *P. W.* 1. 241 ; 3. 237.

Ditty, n. *A simple but often solemn song.* Milton emphasizes the importance of the words. Cf. " smooth-dittied," applied to the music of Lawes, *C.* 86 : *P. L.* 1. 449 ; 11. 584 ; *L.* 32 ; *P.W.* 1. 8 ; 3. 476.

Divinely-warbled, v. adj. *Sung by the celestial choirs* : *H.* 96.

Divisions, n. pl. *Florid, melodic passages* : *P. W.* 3. 62.

Doni, It. n. *Giovanni Battista Doni,* a musician and scholar, contemporary with Milton : *P. W.* 3. 499. See p. 22.

Dorian, adj. *In the Dorian mode of Greek music,* hence, *grave and noble* : *P. L.* 1. 550 ; *P. R.* 4. 257.

Doric, adj. a. *Dorian* (q. v.) : *P. W.* 2. 73.

b. " Doric lay," *pastoral song* : *L.* 189.

Drone, n. *Monotonous sound of a plain-song, or set theme* : *P. W.* 3. 62.

Druides, L. n. pl.: *Ad Mans.* 41 ; 42.   See *Druids.*

Druids, n. pl.   *Ancient Celtic bards* : *L.* 53.

Drum, n.   1. As a signal : *P. W.* 2. 45.

2. In barbaric rites : *P. L.* 1. 394.

Dulcet, adj.   *Sweet to the ear* : *P. L.* 1. 712.   See *sweet.*

Dulcimer, n.   *A wind-instrument similar to the bag-pipe* : *P. L.* 7. 596.   Milton probably took the name from the English version of Daniel 3. 5, 10, 15, where, however, it is a mistranslation of " symphony."   Cf. Revised Version.

Ebur, L. n.   *The ivory plectrum, used for playing the lyre* : *E.* 6. 43.

Echo, 1. v.   a. tr.   *Repeat in manner of an echo* : *P. L.* 5. 873.

b. intr.   *Resound* : *L'A.* 56.

2. n.   a. *Repercussion of sound* : *P. L.* 10. 861 ; *H.* 100 ; *P.* 53 ; *L.* 47.

b. *A nymph who loved Narcissus* : *C.* 230; 275.

Echoing, v. adj.   *Giving back sound* : *P. L.* 4. 681 ; 9. 1107.

Enchanting, v. adj.   With suggestion of *singing* : *L.* 59 ; *P. R.* 2. 158.   Cf. *charming* (1).

Erato, L. n.   *The muse of lyric and amorous poetry* : *E.* 6. 51.

Even-song, n.   *Il P.* 64.

Fancied, adj.   *Fanciful* : *P. W.* 3. 476.

Fancies, n. pl.   *Fantasies,* instrumental compositions of a free and informal type, producing the effect of improvisation.   Possibly with some suggestion of this meaning : *P. L.* 5. 296.

Fiddler, n.   A term of contempt with Milton.   " Municipal fiddler," *a travelling musician* : *P. W.* 2. 73.

Flourish, n.   *A loud trumpet-call* : Fig., *P. W.* 1. 20 ; 92 ; 106 ; 137.

Flute, n.   Regarded by Milton as of the ancient Greek style (see p. 40) : *P. L.* 1. 551 ; *C.* 173 ; *L.* 33.

Fret, n.   *A small ridge set across the finger-board of a stringed instrument to mark the stopping-place for a particular note* : *P. L.* 7. 597.

Fugue, n.   *A composition for the organ in canon form* (see p. 47-48): *P. L.* 11. 563 ; *P. W.* 3. 476.

Gamut, n.   *The musical scale,* hence, *the compass or range of an instrument.*   Used contemptuously : *P. W.* 2. 73.

Grate, v.   1. tr.   *Produce harsh sounds by friction of surfaces* : *P. L.* 2. 881.

2. intr.   *Sound harshly* : *L.* 124.

Guitar, n.   *A six-stringed instrument of the lute class* of Spanish origin : *P. W.* 2. 73.

Hallelu, n.   *Praise* : *S. M.* 18 (*variant*).   See *hallelujah.*

Hallelujah, n. *Song of praise to God* : *P. L.* 2. 243 ; 6. 744 ; 7. 634 ; 10. 642 ; *P. W.* 2. 418 ; 479. Cf. *hallelu.*

Harmonia, L. n. *Harmony*, daughter of Jove and Electra : *De Sphaer. Con.* App. IV, p. 134, l. 14 (see n.).

Harmony, n. 1. *A fitting or adjustment of parts*, hence,

    a. *System in music* : *P. R.* 4. 255 ; *V. Ex.* 51 ; *H.* 107 ; 131 ; *P. W.* 1. 232 ; 279.

    b. Fig., *agreement, order* : *P. L.* 8. 384 ; 605 ; 10. 358 ; *P. W.* 2. 90 ; 3. 207.

    c. *Melody which follows a definite system* : *P. L.* 7. 560 ; *A.* 63 ; *C.* 243 ; *P. W.* 3. 476.

    d. Personified : *P. L.* 5. 625 ; *L'A.* 144.

    2. *Musical concord* : *P. L.* 2. 552 ; 6. 65 ; fig., *P. W.* 3. 346.

Harp, 1. v. intr. *Play upon a harp* : *H.* 115 ; *P. W.* 2. 479.

    2. n. *Hebrew stringed instrument of accompaniment* : *P. L.* 2. 548 ; 3. 365 ; 366 ; 5. 151 ; 7. 258 ; 559 ; 594 ; 11. 560 ; 583 ; *P. R.* 4. 336 ; *Ps.* 81. 8 ; *S. M.* 13.

    3. *The lyre of classical mythology* : *P. L.* 7. 37 ; *P.W.* 3. 467.

    4. *Poetic composition.* The harp is here analogous with the conventional lyre : *P. L.* 3. 414 ; *P.* 9.

    5. *Music sung to the accompaniment of the harp* : *P. L.* 7. 450.

Harsh, adj. *Discordant* : *P. L.* 2. 882 ; *S. A.* 662 ; *C.* 477 ; *S. M.* 20.

High, adj. 1. *Complicated in musical proportions* : *P. L.* 11. 562.

    2. *Sublime* : *Il P.* 163 ; *L.* 87 ; *P. W.* 2. 418.

Hit, v. tr. *Strike a note, with hand or voice* : *P. R.* 4. 255 ; *A.* 77.

Horn, n. *L'A.* 53 ; *A.* 57 ; fig., *L.* 28.

Hosanna, n. Milton emphasizes the Hebrew meaning, " Save, now " : *P. L.* 3. 348 ; 6. 205 ; *P.W.* 1. 316 ; 2. 489 (two reff.).

Hubbub, n. *P. L.* 2. 951 ; 12. 60.

Hymenaean, n. *Marriage hymn* : *P. L.* 4. 711. Cf. *E.* 5. 105-106.

Hymn, 1. v. a. tr. *Celebrate in sacred song* : *P. L.* 4. 944 ; 6. 96.

    b. intr. *Sing sacred songs of praise* : *P. L.* 7. 258.

    2. n. *Sacred song.*

        a. Christian : *P. L.* 2. 242 ; 3. 148 ; 5. 656 ; 6. 745 ; *P. R.* 1. 169 ; 4. 335 ; *H.* 17 ; *S. M.* 15 ; *S.* 13. 11 ; *Ps.* 81. 5 ; *P. W.* 2. 418 ; 479 (2) ; 3. 57 (two reff.) ; 152.

        b. Pagan : *P. R.* 4. 341 ; *P. W.* 1. 125 ; 2. 479 (1).

Innumerable, adj. *Without number.* Hence also *transcending the laws of musical number* : *P. L.* 3. 147. Cf. " inenarrabile carmen," *Ad P.* 37. See *numerous.*

Insonare, L. v. intr. *Sound* : *E.* 6. 38. See *sonare.*

Instrument, n. *P. L.* 11. 559 ; *P. W.* 1. 232 ; 462.

Instrumental, adj. *Made by musical instruments* : *P. L.* 4. 686 ; 6. 65.

Jangle, v. intr. *Sound discordantly* : *P. W.* 1. 167.

Jangling, v. adj. *Discordant* : *P. L.* 12. 55 ; *P. W.* 3. 56.

Jar, v. intr. *Sound discordantly* : *S. M.* 20 ; fig., *P. L.* 5. 793 ; *P. W.* 2. 126.

Jarring, v. adj. *Discordant* : *P. L.* 2. 880 ; 6. 315 ; *P. W.* 2. 474 ; fig., *P. W.* 2. 370.

Jig, n. 1. *A light and lively rustic dance* : *C.* 952 ; *P. W.* 1. 323.
2. *The music of such a dance* : *P. W.* 3. 158.

Jocund, adj. *Gay, lively* : *P. L.* 1. 787 ; *L'A.* 94 ; *C.* 173.

Jubilant, adj. *Rejoicing with songs and shouts* : *P. L.* 7. 564.

Jubilee, n. *Joyful shout, of a sacred character* : *P. L.* 3. 348 ; 6. 884 ; *S. M.* 9.

Lawes, n. *Henry Lawes,* the composer : *S.* 13 (*title*). See App. II.

Lay, n. *Song.* a. Of the nightingale : *P. L.* 7. 436 ; *S.* 1. 8.
b. Of a pastoral character : *C.* 849 ; *L.* 44 ; 189.

Linkèd, v. adj. *Having a melodic connection or progress according to the laws of music* : *L'A.* 140.

Liquid, adj. Describing pure, clear, rippling tones : *S.* 1. 5 ; *P. L.* 7. 68 ; 8. 263.

Lofty, adj. *Solemn, sublime* : *L.* 11 ; *Ps.* 81. 10.

Loud, adj. Describing musical sounds : *P. L.* 1. 394 ; 532 ; 2. 921 ; 5. 193 ; 6. 59 ; 12. 229 ; *S. A.* 1510 ; *H.* 115 ; 215 ; *S. M.* 11 ; *Il P.* 126 ; *V. Ex.* 24 ; *L.* 17.

Loud-sounding, v. adj. : *P. W.* 1. 232.

Low, adj. *In simple musical proportions* : *P. L.* 11. 562. Cf. *high* (1).

Lull, v. tr. *Compose to sleep or rest as with a lullaby* : *P. L.* 2. 287 ; 4. 771 ; *L'A.* 116 ; *A.* 69 ; *V. Ex.* 84.

Lute, n. 1. The most popular stringed instrument of Milton's day. It was similar to the guitar, but with a pear-shaped back, no ribs, and a shorter neck. The finger-board was fretted, and the instrument was played by plucking the strings with the fingers. The number of strings varied : *P. L.* 5. 151 ; *P.* 28 ; *S.* 20. 11; *P. W.* 2. 73 ; 3. 476.
2. *The ancient lyre* : *C.* 478. Cf. *Ad Leon.* 2. 6 ; and see *lyra* (2), *lyre*.

Lydian, adj. *In the Lydian mode,* hence, *soft, effeminate, passionate* : *L'A.* 136.

Lyra, L. n. 1. *The ancient lyre* : *Epit. Dam.* 218.
2. *The lute* : *Ad Leon.* 2. 6. See *lute* (2), *lyre*.

Lyre, n. The most important stringed instrument of antiquity. Used by bards as accompaniment to their chanting, and played either with a plectrum (ψάλλειν), or with the fingers (πλήσσειν, κρέκειν, κρούειν) : *P. L.* 3. 17. See *barbitos, cetra, chelys, cithara, harp, lute* (2), *lyra, pecten*.

Lyric, adj. *Sung to the accompaniment of the lyre* : *P. R.* 4. 257 ; *S. A.* 1737.

Madrigal, n. a. *Part-song, written in counterpoint, without instrumental accompaniment* : *P. W.* 2. 73.

      b. *Pastoral song* (with implied reference to Henry Lawes) : C. 495.

Masque, n. *A form of theatrical entertainment of which music constituted a part* : *L'A.* 128 ; *P. L.* 4. 768 ; fig., *P.* 19 ; *S.* 22. 13. Cf. *Arcades, Comus*.

Matin, 1. n. *Morning song* : *L'A.* 114 ; *P. W.* 2. 476.

      2. adj. *Sounding in the morning* : *P. L.* 5. 7 ; 6. 526 ; 7. 450.

Mean, n. *A tone between two other tones, forming with them a triad.* Possibly with a suggestion of this meaning : *S. A.* 207.

Measure, n. 1. *A solemn and sublime dance* : *P. R.* 1. 170.

      2. *Rhythm* : *P. L.* 9. 846 ; *P. W.* 2. 418 ; 3. 135.

Measured, v. adj. *Rhythmical* : *A.* 71. See *various-measured, well-measured, measure*.

Melesigenes, n. *Homer*, represented as a bard : *P. R.* 4. 259.

Melodious, adj. *Musical* : *P. L.* 3. 371 ; 5. 196 ; 5. 656 ; 11. 559 ; *H.* 129 ; *L.* 14 ; *S. M.* 18 ; *V. Ex.* 51 ; *P. W.* 3. 467.

Melody, n. *Music* : *P. L.* 8. 528 ; *P. W.* 1. 232.

Melos, Gr. n. *Song.* Among the Greeks it was always in unison, or at most in octaves, caused by the mixture of men's and boys' voices. Milton seems to use the term thus : *P. W.* 1. 169 : *Ad P.* 37 ; *Ad Sals.* 22 ; *Ad Rous.* 11.

Memoria, L. n. *Memory* (q. v.) : *De Id. Plat.* 3.

Memory, n. *Mnemosyne*, Mother of the Muses : *P. W.* 2. 481.

Metal, n. Used for the trumpet : *P. L.* 1. 540. See *alchymy, sphere-metal*.

Minstrelsy, n. 1. *Pastoral music* : *C.* 547.

      2. *A body of musicians* : *P. L.* 6. 168.

Mode, s. v. *Mood*.

Modulamen, L. n. *Melody* : *Ad P.* 50.

Modulare, L. v. intr. *Play or sing a tune* : *E.* 5. 113 ; 6. 85 ; *Ad Mans.* 30.

Modulus, L. n. *A strain of music* : *E.* 6. 7 ; *Ad P.* 59.

Modus, L. n. *Mode, melody* : *E.* 2. 23 ; *Epit. Dam.* 89. See *mood*.

Mood, n. *The Greek scale of eight tones.* Seven varieties are usually distinguished — the Mixolydian, Lydian, Phrygian, Dorian, Hypolydian, Ionian or Hypophrygian, Aeolian or Hypodorian. Hence, *a melody or tune* : *P. L.* 1. 550 ; *L.* 87 ; *S. A.* 662 ; *P. W.* 1. 460. See *Modus.*

Morrice, n. *The morrice-dance.* In Milton's time it had degenerated into a disorderly revel, and was suppressed by the Puritans along with the May games and other " enticements unto naughtiness " : *C.* 116 ; *P. W.* 3. 152.

Motion, n. 1. *Movement productive of sound.*

        a. Of the heavenly bodies : *P. L.* 3. 582 ; 5. 625 ; 7. 500 ; 8. 35 ; 115 ; 130 ; 10. 658 ; *A.* 71.

        b. Used abstractly : *U. C.* 2. 7 ; 8. Cf. *P. L.* 5. 580-582.

    2. *Melodic progression in song* : *S. M.* 22. See *move.*

Move, v. 1. a. tr. Of the heavenly bodies, as productive of sound : *P. L.* 3. 579 ; 8. 130 ; 132.

        b. intr. *P. L.* 3. 719 ; 5. 177 ; 8. 33 ; 70 ; 10. 652.

    2. intr. *Change from one tone to another* : *H.* 129. See *motion.*

Murmur, 1. v. intr. *Give forth soft musical sounds* : *Il P.* 144.

    2. n. *Soft musical sound* : *P. L.* 2. 284 ; 5. 196 ; 7. 68 ; *P. R.* 4. 248.

Murmuring, v. adj. *Sounding softly and musically* : *P. L.* 4. 260 ; 453 ; 8. 263.

Musa, L. n. *A Muse* (q. v.) : *E.* 1. 25 ; 69 ; 2. 18 ; 4. 51 ; 5. 30 ; 6. 3 ; 22 ; *Ad P.* 5 ; 56 ; *Ad Sals.* 31 ; *Ad Mans.* 9 ; 55 ; *Epit. Dam.* 13 ; 126. Cf. *De Id. Plat.* 1-3 ; *Ad Mans.* 2. See *Camoena.*

Musaeus, n. *Mythical Greek poet and musician* : *Il P.* 104.

Muse, n. 1. *One of the nine goddesses, the daughters of Zeus and Mnemosyne* (see *Memory*) *who presided over the liberal arts* : *P. L.* 3. 27 ; 7. 6 ; 37 ; *Il P.* 47 ; *L.* 58 ; 59 ; *S.* 1. 13 ; 8. 9 ; *P. W.* 1. 115 ; 3. 140 ; 488 (two reff.) ; 502.

    2. *The power that inspires poetry, personified* : *P. L.* 1. 6 ; 376 ; 3. 19 ; *P.* 4 ; *C.* 515 ; *L.* 133 ; *H.* 15 ; *V. Ex.* 53.

    3. *Poetry* : *L.* 66 ; *P. W.* 3. 489.

    4. *Poet, bard* : *L.* 19. Cf. " dame Memory and her siren daughters " : *P. W.* 2. 481. See *Camoena, Clio, Erato, Musa, Thalia, Urania.*

Music, n. 1. *The art of the rhythmic and harmonic combination of tones* : *A.* 68 ; *S.* 13. 2 ; *P. W.* 1. 255 ; 3. 61 ; 476.

    2. *Melody or harmony in general* : *P. L.* 1. 787 ; 5. 548 ; 11. 592 ; *P. R.* 4. 332 ; *H.* 93 ; 117 ; *Il P.* 151 ; *A.* 74 ; *S. M.* 21 ; *P.* 1 ; *Cir.* 2 ; *P. W.* 2. 73.

Musical, adj. 1. *Skilled in music* : *P. W.* 3. 488.

    2. *Consisting of music* : *P. W.* 3. 499.

    3. *Melodious* : *C.* 478 ; *Il P.* 62.

Musician, n. : *P. W.* 1. 58.

Nightingale, n. : *P. L.* 4. 602 ; 771 ; 5. 41 ; 7. 435 ; *C.* 234 ; 566 ; *S.* 1. 1. Cf. " Bird of night " : *P. L.* 8. 518. See *Attic bird, Philomel.*

Night-warbling, v. adj. *P. L.* 5. 40. See *warbling.*

Noise, n. 1. *A band of musicians, or its music* : *H.* 97 ; *S. M.* 18 ; possibly, *P. L.* 1. 394 ; 8. 243 ; *Il P.* 61.

    2. *Confused sound, usually loud* : *P. L.* 1. 498 ; 2. 896 ; 957 ; 6. 211 ; 667 ; 12. 55 ; *S. A.* 1508 ; 1509 ; 1511 ; *C.* 170 ; *S.* 12. 3.

    3. *Sound in general* : *P. L.* 2. 64 ; 6. 487 ; 10. 567 ; *C.* 369.

Note, n. 1. *Musical character representing a tone* : *S.* 13. 3.

    2. *Musical tone* : *P. L.* 2. 494 ; 548 ; 3. 17 : 40 ; 4. 683 ; 5. 199 ; 9. 6 ; *P. R.* 4. 246 ; 437 ; *P. 9* ; *H.* 116 ; *L'A.* 134 ; 139 ; *Il P.* 106 ; *S.* 1. 5 ; 20. 12 ; *P. W.* 1. 367.

Number, 1. v. tr. *Regulate* : *U. C.* 2. 7 ; 8.

    2. n. *Mathematical element in music.* Hence, *rhythm, musical measure* : *P. L.* 3. 38 ; 346 ; 580 ; *P. R.* 4. 255 ; *On Shakes.* 10.

Numerous, adj. *Regulated by number, rhythmical* : *P. L.* 5. 150 ; *P. W.* 3. 117. See *innumerable.*

Oat, n. *Shepherd's pipe* : *L.* 88. See *arundo, cicuta, pipe, reed.*

Oaten, adj. *Made of the stem of the oat* : *L.* 33 ; *C.* 345.

Ode, n. *Elaborate lyric poem expressive of exalted or enthusiastic emotion, intended to be sung.* Milton probably had in mind the triumphant songs of Pindar : *P. R.* 1. 182 ; 4. 257 ; *H.* 24 ; *P. W.* 2. 57 ; 479.

Organ, n. 1. The organ of Milton's day was an elaborate structure and capable of producing a great variety of sounds. A typical example was the organ at York Cathedral, built by Robert Dallam, and presented by Charles I. " Every stop contained 51 pipes, so we may conclude that the semitones were divided ; it had a great organ of nine stops and choir organ of five, and three pairs of bellows, but no pedals, for pedals seem to have been unknown in England until the last decade of the eighteenth century." (C. F. A. Williams, *Story of the Organ,* 1903, p. 108) : *P. L.* 1. 708 ; 7. 596 ; 11. 560 ; *H.* 130 ; *Il P.* 161 ; *P. W.* 3. 476.

    2. *Wind-instruments in general* : *P. L.* 7. 596.

Organist, n. : *P. W.* 3. 476.

Orpheus, n. *The Thracian singer, son of Calliope* : *P. L.* 3. 17 · *L'A.* 145 ; *Il P.* 105 ; *L.* 58 ; *P. W.* 3. 467 ; *Ad P.* 52.

Paean, L. n. *Apollo as god of music* : *Ad Sals.* 25.   See *Apollo, Delius, Phoebus.*

Pan, n.   *The sylvan god,* as a lover of music : *P. L.* 4. 266 ; *C.* 176 ; 268 ; *Epit. Dam.* 52 ; *S.* 13. 6 (*variant*).

Part, n.   *The melody given to a voice or instrument in a concerted piece of music* : *P. L.* 3. 371.

Partial, adj.   *Sung independently, without concerted harmony,* hence, *selfish* : *P. L.* 2. 552.

Pastoral, adj.   *Pertaining to shepherds and their music* : *P. L.* 11. 132 ; *C.* 345.

Peal, 1. v. tr.   *Assail with loud, metallic sounds* : *P. L.* 2. 920.
    2. n.   *Loud, metallic sound.*
        a. Of the trumpet : *P. L.* 3. 329.
        b. Of the barking of dogs : *P. L.* 2. 656.
        c. Of a volley of words : *S. A.* 235 ; 906.

Pealing, v. adj.   Of the sound of the trumpet-stops in an organ : *Il P.* 161.

Pecten, L. n.   *Plectrum for playing the ancient lyre.* By synechdoche, *the lyre itself.* Hence, fig., *poetry or song* : *Ad Rous.* 10.   Cf. *plectrum.*

Personating, v. adj.   *Sounding forth* : *P. R.* 4. 341.

Philomel, n.   *The nightingale* (q. v.) : *Il P.* 56.   See also *Attic bird, Philomela.*

Philomela, L. n. : *E.* 5. 25.   See *Philomel.*

Phoebus, n. 1.   *Apollo as god of music and poetry* : *P. R.* 4. 260 ; *L.* 77 ; *S.* 13. 10 ; *E.* 6. 15 ; 33 ; 45 ; *Ad P.* 64 ; *Ad Sals.* 24 *Ad Rous.* 63 ; *Ad Mans.* 2 ; 24 ; 35 ; 38 (two reff.).   See *Apollo, Delius, Paean.*
    2. *Song, poetry* : *P.* 23.

Pipe, 1. v. intr.   *Play on a pipe* : *C.* 823 ; fig., *Il P.* 126.
    2. n.   *An organ-pipe* : *P. L.* 1. 709.
    3. *The pastoral wind-instrument* : *P. L.* 11. 132 ; *P. R.* 1. 480 *C.* 173 ; *L.* 124 ; *S.* 13. 6 (*variant*).
    4. *A flute* : *P. L.* 1. 561 ; 7. 595 ; *P. R.* 2. 363 ; *S. A.* 1616 ; *P. W.* 3. 184.   See *arundo, cicuta, oat, reed.*

Pitch, n.   *The position of any sound in the musical scale* : *P. W.* 1. 232.

Plain-song, n.   *A theme on which variations can be played, or to which harmonies may be added* : *P. W.* 3. 62.

Play, v. intr.   *To make music* : *P. L.* 7. 10.

Plectrum, L. n.   *A small piece of ivory or metal sometimes used for playing the ancient lyre* : *E.* 6. 43 ; *Ad P.* 33.   Cf. *pecten.*

Prattle, v. intr. *Utter a continuous tinkling sound* : *P. W.* 2. 73.

Preamble, n. *Musical prelude* : *P. L.* 3. 367.

Prelude, n. *Introduction to a musical composition* : *P. W.* 1. 245.

Proaemium, L. n. In Greek music, *the prelude* : *P. W.* 1. 232.

Proem, n. Shortened form of *proaemium* (q. v.) : *P. L.* 9. 549.

Proportion, 1. v. tr. *Regulate according to the laws of harmony* : *S. A.* 209.

    2. n. *Mathematical relation of intervals and rhythm in music* : *P. L.* 11. 562 ; fig., *P. L.* 8. 385. See *disproportion, disproportioned, proportional, well-proportioned*, and the explanations given above, p. 138.

Proportional, adj. *Harmonious* : fig., *P. W.* 2. 90.

Psallere (Gr. ψάλλειν), L. v. intr. *Play upon a stringed instrument with a plectrum* : *E.* 6. 43.

Psalm, n. *Sacred song* : *P. R.* 4. 335 ; *S. M.* 15.

Psalmistry, n. *Singing of psalms* : *P. W.* 1. 325.

Psaltery, n. *Ancient Hebrew stringed instrument* : *Ps.* 81. 7.

Quill, n. *Shepherd's pipe* : *L.* 188.

Quire, n. See *choir*.

Rebeck, n. *A primitive, shrill-toned, rustic fiddle* : *L'A.* 94 ; *P.W.* 2. 73.

Recorder, n. *A flute or flageolet, similar to the ancient Greek instrument* : *P. L.* 1. 551.

Reed, n. *Pastoral pipe* : *P. L.* 11. 132 ; *C.* 345 ; *L.* 86. See *arundo, cicuta, oat, pipe*.

Resonant, adj. *Repeating the same theme again and again* : *P. L.* 11. 563. See *resounding* (2).

Resound, v. a. tr. *Sound again, re-echo* : *P.L.* 2. 789 ; 3. 149 ; 10. 862.

    b. intr. : *P. L.* 1. 315 ; 6. 218 ; 10. 862 ; *P. R.* 2. 290 : *H.* 182.

Resounding, v. adj. 1. *Echoing* : *H.* 182.

    2. *Re-echoing, as in counterpoint* : *C.* 243. See *resonant*.

Responsories, n. pl. *Musical answers in the church service* : *P. W.* 1. 460 ; 2. 61.

Responsive, adj. *Singing in parts or in the manner of a duet* : *P. L.* 4. 683.

Ring, 1. v. tr. *Sound, as of vibrating metal* : *P. L.* 2. 655 ; 6. 204 ; *L'A.* 114 ; *Ps.* 81. 4.

    2. intr. *Give the sound of vibrating metal* : *H.* 125 ; *L'A.* 93.

    3. intr. *Resound, reverberate* : *P. L.* 2. 495 ; 723 ; 3. 347 ; 7. 562 ; 633 ; 9. 737 ; *H.* 158 ; *P.* 2 ; fig., *S. A.* 1449 ; *S.* 15. 1 ; 22. 12.

    4. n. *Sound produced by striking metal* : *H.* 208.

Roar, 1. v. intr. *Make a loud sound* : P. L. 2. 267 ; 6. 871 ; 11. 713 ; *P. R.* 4. 463 ; *C.* 87 ; *V. Ex.* 86.

    2. n. *Full, deep sound* : P. L. 6. 586 ; *P. R.* 4. 428 ; *Il P.* 76.

    3. n. *Confused, loud sound* : *C.* 549 ; *L.* 61.

Round, 1. v. intr. *Pace about to the sound of music* : P. L. 4. 685.

    2. n. *A dance with accompanying song* : P. L. 8. 125 ; *C.* 114 ; 144.

Roundel, n. *A popular song in canon form* : *P. W.* 2. 57.

Rule, n. *Mathematical law in music* : P. L. 5. 297.

Sacred, adj. Applied to music : P. L. 3. 29 ; 149 ; 369 ; *Ps.* 87. 26.

Scrannel, adj. *Making a thin, rasping sound* : *L.* 124.

Serenate, n. *Serenade, love-song* : P. L. 4. 769.

Service, n. *Religious worship accompanied by music* : *Il P.* 163 ; *H.* 244.

Set, v. tr. *Put words to music* : *P. W.* 2. 73.

Shout, 1. v. intr. *Cry aloud in exultation* : *S. A.* 1473.

    2. n. *Loud outcry* : P. L. 1. 542 ; 2. 520 ; 3. 345 ; 6. 96 ; 200 ; 7. 256 ; 10. 505 ; *S. A.* 1472 ; 1510 ; 1620 ; *C.* 103 ; *S. M.* 9.

Shrill, adj. P. L. 5. 7 ; *L'A.* 56.

Sigh, v. intr. P. L. 2. 788 ; 9. 783.

Sighing, v. n. *H.* 186.

Signal, n. *Musical call, inciting to action* : P. L. 1. 278 ; 347 ; 776 ; 2. 717 ; 11. 72 ; 12. 593.

Sing, v. I. tr. 1. *Express in rhythmical form.*

        a. Of Milton's own poetry : *P. R.* 1. 1 ; 2.

        b. Of poetry or verse : *A.* 29 ; *S. A.* 203 ; *Ps.* 7. 63 ; *P. W.* 2. 479 ; 3. 118.

        c. Of prophecy : P. L. 12. 324 ; *P. R.* 3. 178.

    2. *Chant to instrumental accompaniment.*

        a. Of bards : *V. Ex.* 37 ; *Il P.* 105 ; 117 ; *S. A.* 983.

        b. Of the celestial choirs : P. L. 2. 242 ; 547 ; 3. 372 ; 383 ; 4. 684 ; 711 ; 5. 405 ; 6. 744 ; 886 (two reff.) ; 7. 182 ; 259 ; 275 ; 565 ; 601 ; 10. 642 ; 12. 367 ; *P. R.* 4. 506 ; 594 ; 637 ; *Circ.* 4 ; *S. M.* 7 ; 16 ; *P. W.* 2. 418.

        c. Of celebration in general : P. L. 5. 148 ; *P. R.* 4. 339 ; *P. W.* 3. 344. See *canere, cantare.*

    3. *Utter by means of a set melody* : P. L. 4. 769 ; 11. 583 ; *P. W.* 1. 462 ; 2. 73.

    4. *Utter melodiously.* Of the nightingale : P. L. 4. 603 ; 8. 519.

    II. intr. 1. *Express thought in rhythmical form.*

        a. Of Milton's own poetry ; P. L. 3. 18 ; 7. 24 ; *V. Ex.* 45.

    b. Of poetry in general : *L'A.* 17 ; 49 ; *P. W.* 3. 331.

    c. Of prophecy : *P. L.* 12. 244 ; *H.* 5.

  2. *Chant to instrumental accompaniment.*

    a. Of a bard : *P. R.* 4. 258 ; *L.* 10 ; 11 ; 186.

    b. Of the Muses ; *P. L.* 1. 6 ; *Il P.* 48 ; *P.* 4.

    c. Of the celestial choirs : *P. L.* 2. 553 ; 7. 192 ; 573 ; 633 ;
       10. 643 ; *P. R.* 1. 171 ; 172 ; 243 ; *H.* 119 ; *S. M.* 28;
       L. 179 ; 180 ; *Ps.* 5. 35.

    d. Of the sirens on the spheres : *A.* 65.

    e. Of Circe and her sirens : *C.* 256.

    f. Of the Hesperides : *C.* 983. See *canere, cantare.*

  3. *Utter words to a set melody* : *P. L.* 11. 619 ; *S.* 13. 13 ; *V.*

Ex. 63 ; *Ps.* 81. 1 ; 2 ; 87. 25.

    4. *Make melodious sounds.*

    a. Of birds : *P. L.* 3. 39 ; 5. 198 ; *L'A.* 7 ; 42 ; *S.* 1. 9 ; 11.

    b. Of the bee : *Il P.* 143.

    c. Of stringed instruments : *P. R.* 1. 172.

    d. Of the trumpet : *P. L.* 6. 526. See *song.*

Singing-robes, n. *Choristers' garments* : *P. W.* 2. 477.

Siren, n. 1. *One of the nymphs who bewitched men by their singing* :
C. 253 ; 878 ; *P. W.* 3. 517.

  2. *A female singer, sitting one upon each of the nine spheres,
" sounding a single note "*: *A.* 63 ; *S. M.* 1.

  3. *One of the Muses,* possibly as identified with the sirens of
the spheres : *P. W.* 2. 481.

Sirena, L. n. *Siren of the spheres*: *De Sphaer. Con.,* App. IV, p. 133,
1. 3. See *Siren* (2).

Soft, adj. *P. L.* 1. 551 ; 561 ; 7. 436 ; 598 ; 11. 584 ; 848 ; *L'A.*
136 ; *C.* 86 ; 259 ; 555 ; *L.* 44 ; *P.* 27 ; *S.* 1. 8.

Sole, adj. *Singing solo parts* : *P. L.* 4. 683.

Solemn-breathing, v. adj. Of vocal music : *C.* 555. See *breathe.*

Sol-fa, n. *A system of syllables for singing the musical scale* : *P.
W.* 2. 86.

Sonare, L. v. intr. *Sound* : *E.* 4. 118 ; 5. 21 ; *Epit. Dam.* 61; 120; 155.
See *insonare.*

Song, n. 1. *Expression of thought in rhythmical form.*

    a. Of Milton's own poetry : *P. L.* 1. 13 ; 3. 413 ; 7. 30 ;
       9. 25 ; *P. R.* 1. 12 ; *H.* 239 ; *P.* 8 ; *M. M.* 9.

    b. Of sublime diction in general : *P. L.* 7. 107 ; 10. 862 ;
       P. W. 1. 60.

    c. Of poetry ; *P. R.* 4. 336 ; 347 ; fig., *P. W.* 3. 453.

    2. *Chant to instrumental accompaniment.*

        a. Of a bard : *V. Ex.* 49 ; *C.* 44.

        b. Of the celestial choirs : *P. L.* 2. 252 ; 3. 148 ; 369 ;
            4. 687 ; 944 ; 5. 161 ; 547 ; 619; 6. 167 ; 10. 648 ;
            P. R. 4. 505 ; *H.* 133 ; *Circ.* 2 ; *S. M.* 6 ; 25 ; *L.* 176 ;
            P. W. 3. 122.

        c. Of dignified singing in general : *P. L.* 1. 441 ; 2. 556 ;
            3. 29 ; 5. 204 ; 7. 12 ; 9. 800 ; *P. R.* 4. 341 ; *Ps.* 81. 5 ;
            87. 26 ; *P. W.* 2. 57 ; 407 ; 3. 58 ; 517. See *carmen.*

    3. *Melody set to words :* *P. L.* 8. 243 ; 11. 594 : *P. R.* 1. 480 ;
S. A. 1737 ; *C.* 86 ; 268 ; 854 ; 878 ; *L.* 36 ; *S.* 13. 1 ; *P. W.* 1.
462 ; 2. 73 ; fig., *P. W.* 1. 450 ; 2. 476. See *cantus.*

    4. *Musical sound.*

        a. Of birds : *P. L.* 5. 7 ; 41 ; 7. 433 ; *P. R.* 2. 281 ; *C.* 235 ·
            Il P. 56.

        b. Of the pipe : *L.* 123.

        c. Of the spheres ; *P. L.* 5. 178. See *sing.*

Sonitus, L. n. *Sound :* *E.* 5. 12. See *sound* (2).

Sonus, L. n. *Sound :* *Ad Leon.* 1. 8 ; *Ad P.* 4 ; *Epit. Dam.* 159.
See *sound* (2).

Sound, 1. v. a, tr. *Announce by a sound :* *P. L.* 7. 443.

        b. *Cause to sound :* *P. L.* 6. 202.

        c. *Proclaim :* *P. L.* 5. 172.

        d. intr. *Give forth sound :* *P. L.* 6. 204 ; 11. 76 ; *P.* 26 ;
            L'A. 94 ; *Il P.* 74.

    2. n. Of musical instruments, or of the voice : *P. L.* 1. 531 ;
540 ; 711 ; 754 ; 2. 286 ; 476 ; 515 ; 880 ; 952 ; 3. 147 ; 4. 453 ;
686 ; 5. 5 ; 872 ; 6. 64 ; 97 ; 749 ; 829 ; 7. 206 ; 558 ; 597 ; 8.
243 ; 606 ; 9. 451 ; 518 ; 10. 642 ; 11. 558 ; 12. 229 ; *P. R.*
1. 19 ; 2. 403 ; 4. 17 ; 247 ; *C.* 345 ; 555 ; 942 ; *H.* 53 ; 101 ;
A. 78 ; *L.* 35 ; *S. M.* 3 ; *Ps.* 81. 10 ; *V. Ex.* 32 ; *P. W.* 3. 117 ;
273 ; 522. See *sonitus, sonus.*

Sound-board, n. In an organ, " *a structure consisting of grooves,
channels, upper-board, table, and sliders, placed above the wind-
chest* " (C. F. A. Williams, *Story of the Organ,* 1903, p. 270. Cf.
the figure, *ibid.,* p. 17) : *P. L.* 1. 709.

Sounding, v. adj. *Giving forth sounds :* *P. L.* 1. 668 ; 2. 517 ; *L.* 154.

Span, v. tr. fig., *Fit together, match,* in setting music to words :
S. 13. 2.

Sphere, n. In the Pythagorean astronomy, *one of the orbs or hollow
globes, in which the heavenly bodies were set, revolving about the
earth as a common centre, and giving forth sounds inaudible to*

human ears : *P. L.* 5. 169 ; 6. 315 ; *H.* 125 ; *A.* 64 ; *C.* 113. See *De Sphaer. Con.*, App. IV.

Sphere-born, v. adj. *Descended from the spheres* : *S. M.* 2.

Sphere-metal, n. *The material of which the spheres are composed, through whose vibration musical sounds are produced* : *U. C.* 2. 5.

Sphery, adj. *Of the spheres* : *C.* 1021.

Stop, n. 1. In a flute or pipe, *one of the holes stopped by the fingers, by which the pitch is regulated* : *P. L.* 7. 596 ; *C.* 345 ; *L.* 188.

2. Correspondingly, in the organ, *the mechanism for regulating the sound by " stopping " the pipes.* For an explanation of this mechanism, and its history, see C. F. A. Williams, *Story of the Organ*, 1903, pp. 31 ; 61-62 ; 267 : *P. L.* 7. 596 ; 11. 561 ; *P. W.* 3. 476. Cf. *Epit. Dam.* 135.

Strain, n. *Quality of melody or verse* : *P. L.* 5. 148 ; *H.* 17 ; *L'A.* 148; *C.* 494 ; 561 ; *L.* 87 ; fig., *Il P.* 174 ; *P. W.* 1. 25 ; 357 ; 369 ; 2. 57 ; 418 ; 3. 141.

Strepitus, L. n. *The sound of the lyre* : *Ad Mans.* 63.

String, n. *Vibrating cord or wire of a musical instrument.*

　　a. When Milton speaks of " the string " or " strings " in general, he has in mind the classic lyre, or its Scriptural counterpart, the harp : *P. L.* 7. 597 ; *P. R.* 2. 363 ; *A.* 87 ; *H.* 97 ; *Il P.* 106 ; *L.* 17 ; *Ps.* 81. 8.

　　b. Of the lute and viol : *P.* 27. See *chord* (1), *wire.*

Style, n. *Manner of musical expression* : *P. L.* 5. 146.

Sweep, v. tr. *Move the hand as in playing the lyre* : *L.* 17.

Sweet, adj. *P. L.* 1. 712 ; 3. 346 ; 367 ; 7. 596 ; 9. 321 ; *S. A.* 1737 ; *H.* 93 ; *Il P.* 56 ; 151 ; *C.* 249 ; 878 ; *Circ.* 4 ; *V. Ex.* 63. See *dulcet.*

Symphonious, adj. *Concordant* : *P. L.* 7. 559.

Symphony, n. 1. The Greek συμφωνία, *a concord of two sounds*, i. e., a fourth, a fifth, or an octave. Hence, *musical concord, in general* : *P. L.* 1. 712 ; 3. 368 ; 5. 162 ; 11. 595 ; *H.* 132 ; *S. M.* 11 (*variant*) ; *P. W.* 1. 232.

2. *A band or choir, playing or singing in concord* : *P. W.* 2. 479 ; 3. 476.

Syrinx, n. *An Arcadian nymph,* changed into a reed to escape the god Pan ; *P. R.* 2. 188 ; *A.* 106 ; 107.

Tetrachordon, n. Literally *four-stringed*, a term representing the earliest Greek scale. The tones would be represented in the modern scale by e, f, g, a, the lowest being half a tone below the next, and the others rising in intervals of a whole tone. Milton probably had this primitive four-part " harmony " in mind when he called his second divorce-pamphlet *Tetrachordon*, that is, a harmony of the four chief passages in Scripture on divorce : *S.* 11. 1.

Thalia, L. n. *The Muse of comedy, and later of lyric poetry* : *E.* 6. 48.

Thick-warbled, v. adj. *Containing many trills crowded together* : *P. R.* 4. 246. See *warble*.

Timbrel, n. *An instrument of percussion similar to the tambourine.* In the Bible it is always an instrument of rejoicing ; cf. esp. Job 21. 12, where it is paired with the harp. To Milton, however, it seems to suggest horror and barbaric rites : *P. L.* 1. 394 ; *S. A.* 1617 ; *H.* 219 ; *Ps.* 81. 6.

Time, n. *Musical rhythm* : *H.* 129 ; in pun : *U. C.* 2. 7 ; 8.

Touch, 1. v. tr. *Play.* a. On stringed instruments ; *P. L.* 7. 258 ; *A.* 87 ; *S. M.* 13 ; *S.* 20. 10.

    b. On the stops of wind-instruments : *L.* 188.

    2. n. *The act of playing a musical instrument with the hand* : *P. L.* 4. 686 ; *V. Ex.* 38.

    3. *The pressing of the keys in playing an organ* : *P. L.* 11. 561.

Transverse, adj. *Crossing and re-crossing in seeming confusion* : *P. L.* 11. 563 ; *S. A.* 209.

Trill, v. tr. *To sing quaveringly* : *P. R.* 4. 246.

Triton, n. *The herald of Poseidon,* represented as blowing upon a shell : *C.* 873. Cf. *Nat. non Pat. Sen.* 57-58.

True, adj. *Harmonically accurate* : *C.* 997.

Trump, n. *Trumpet* (q. v.) : *P.* 26 ; *H.* 156.

Trumpet, n. *Wind-instrument of metal, used for signal, or noise of acclaim* : *P. L.* 1. 532 ; 754 ; 2. 515 ; 6. 60 ; 203 ; 526 ; 7. 296 ; 11. 74 ; 12. 229 ; *P. R.* 1. 19 ; *S. A.* 1598 ; *S. M.* 11 (*variants*) ; *H.* 58 ; *Ps.* 81. 10 ; *P. W.* 1. 232 ; 495 ; 2. 91 ; 368 ; 404 ; 474 ; 3. 70 ; 480. See *angel-trumpets, buccina, clarion, tuba.*

Trumpeter, n. : fig., *P. W.* 1. 17.

Tuba, L. n. *Trumpet* (q. v.) : *E.* 3. 60 ; 4. 80.

Tune, 1. v. tr. a. *Utter musically* : *P. L.* 3. 40 ; 5. 41 ; 196 ; 7. 436 ; 559 ; *P. R.* 1. 182 ; fig., *P. L.* 9. 549.

    b. *Set to music* : *S.* 13. 11.

    c. *Put in tune* ; *P. L.* 3. 366 ; fig., *P. W.* 2. 408.

    d. *Adapt* : *P.* 8.

    2. n. a. *A melody* : *S. A.* 661 ; *A.* 72 ; *Il P.* 117.

    b. *Concord* : *S. M.* 26 ; *P. W.* 3. 476.

Tuneable, adj. *Musical* : *P. L.* 5. 151 ; *P. R.* 1. 480.

Tuneful, adj. a. *Melodious* : *S.* 13. 1.

    b. *Producing melody* : *P. R.* 2. 290.

Tuning, v. n.   *Concord* : *P. L.* 7. 598.

Tuscan, adj. " Tuscan air," *the music of Tuscan composers.* Possibly Milton had in mind some of the songs of Monteverde, Luca Marenzio, and others, which he had purchased in Italy : *S.* 20. 12.

Unexpressive, adj.   *Inexpressible* : *H.* 116 ; *L.* 176.

Unison, adj. In vocal music, *the entire chorus singing the same part* : *P. L.* 7. 599.

Unsung, v. adj.   *Not celebrated in song* : *P. L.* 1. 442 ; 7. 21 ; 253 ; 9. 33 ; *P. R.* 1. 17.

Urania, n.   *The Heavenly Muse* (cf. *P. L.* 1. 6), hence, *the divine inspiration for Christian poetry* : *P. L.* 7. 1. 31.

Various, adj.   *Containing a variety of musical sounds or rhythms.* The " various quills " of the shepherd in *Lycidas* are probably suggested by the clustered pipes of the syrinx : *P. L.* 5. 146 ; 8. 125 ; *L.* 188.

Various-measured, v. adj.   *Having a variety of metres* : *P. R.* 4. 256.

Verse, n.   a. *The words in song,* as contrasted with the melody : *P. L.* 5. 150 ; 9. 24 ; *P. R.* 4. 256 ; *L'A.* 137 ; *C.* 516 ; 859 ; *P.* 22 ; 47 ; *H.* 17.

     b. Personified : *S. M.* 2 ; *S.* 13. 9.   See *carmen.*

Viol, n. The generic name of the family of bowed instruments which succeeded the medieval Fiddle and preceded the Violin. Viols were of four sizes, treble or discant, tenor, bass, and double bass. The last named is still in use, with very little modification. Milton's viol was probably the bass viol. (Cf. *Richardson,* page v.) This instrument resembled the modern violoncello rather than the double bass.   The regular number of strings was six, and these were tuned by fourths and thirds, instead of fifths as in the 'cello.   The range of the instrument was parallel to that of the human voice, the lowest note being the low D.

    In Milton's time the bass viol had considerable importance and individuality among musical instruments. It is better known by its Italian name of *Viola da gamba.* The reason for the bass viol's importance is to be found in its similarity to the theorbo lute, in tuning. As a result most lutenists could play on the bass viol as well.   The greater part of the music now extant which was played on the bass viol of the seventeenth century is evidently an adaptation of music for lute or voice.

    The bass viol was the last of the old viol family to disappear from common use.   It kept its place even after the introduction of the violin had forced out the higher forms of viols and it was a popular instrument among the Puritans. (Grove's *Dict.* s. v.

viol, violin.) It is significant that Milton groups the " lute and viol ": *P.* 28.

Violin, n. Possibly *one of the smaller, high-pitched viols.* But Milton may well have in mind the modern instrument, which, in his time, had already won great favor : *P.W.* 2. 73. See *viol.*

Vocal, adj. a. *Consisting of vocal music* : *P. L.* 9. 198.

b. *Filled with sound* : *P. L.* 5. 204 ; 9. 530 ; *C.* 247 ; *L.* 86.

Voice, n. a. Employed in song : *P. L.* 1. 712 ; 3. 347 ; 370 ; 4. 682 ; 7. 24 ; 37 ; 598 ; 9. 199 ; *P. R.* 1. 172 ; 4. 256 ; *S. A.* 1065 ; *H.* 27 ; 96 ; *A.* 77 ; *L'A.* 142 ; *S. M.* 17 ; *S.* 20. 11 ; *P. W.* 3. 476.

b. *The melody in vocal music, personified* : *S. M.* 2.

Volant, adj. *Light, fleeting,* describing the touch of an organist : *P. L.* 11. 561.

Warble, v. 1. tr. a. *Sing like a wild bird* : *L'A.* 134.

b. *Sing in a complicated style* : *L.* 189 ; *Il P.* 106 ; *S.* 20. 12.

c. *Produce liquid sounds, like the rapid notes of a bird* : *P. L.* 5. 195 ; 196.

d. *Celebrate in song* : *Ps.* 136. 89.

2. intr. a. *Sing with trills and quavers* : *P. L.* 7. 436 ; 8. 265 ; *S.* 1. 2.

b. *Produce liquid sound, like a bird-song* : *P. L.* 3. 31.

Warbled, v. adj. 1. *Sung* : *P. L.* 2. 242 ; *C.* 854.

2. *Accompanied with singing* : *A.* 87. See *divinely-warbled, thick-warbled.*

Warbling, v. adj. *Consisting of song* : *S. A.* 934. See *night-warbling.*

Well-measured, v. adj. *Well-proportioned as to rhythm* : *S.* 13. 1.

Well-proportioned, v. adj. *Having correct musical proportions* : *P. W.* 1. 232. See *proportion* (1).

Whisper, 1. v. a. tr. *Utter soft, musical sounds* : *P. L.* 8. 516 ; *H.* 66.

b. intr. *P. L.* 4. 158 ; 326 ; *P. R.* 2. 26.

2. n. *Soft, musical sound* : *L'A.* 136.

Whispering, v. adj. *Uttering soft, musical sounds* : *P. R.* 4. 250 ; *L'A.* 116.

Whistle, 1. v. intr. *L'A.* 64.

2. n. *C.* 346 ; fig., *P. W.* 3. 84.

Wind, v. tr. *Blow* : *L.* 28.

Winding, v. adj. Describing involved melodic progression : *L'A.* 129.

Wire, n. *String of a musical instrument, particularly the lyre or harp* : *P. L.* 7. 597 ; *S. M.* 13 ; *V. Ex.* 38. See *string.*

BIBLIOGRAPHY

1. Biographical-Works

Aubrey, J. *Collections for the Life of John Milton* (1669-1696) in his *Brief Lives*, ed. A. Clark, 2 vols., Oxford, 1898. Cited as Aubrey, *Brief Lives*.

Corson, H. *Introduction to the Prose and Poetical Works of John Milton*, New York, 1899.

Godwin, W. *Lives of Edward and John Philips, Nephews and Pupils of John Milton*, London, 1815. Appendix II contains Edward Philips' *Life of Milton*. Cited as E. Philips, *Life*.

Graham, J. J. G. *Autobiography of John Milton, or Milton's Life in his own Words*, London, 1872.

Keightley, T. *An Account of the Life, Opinions and Writings of John Milton*, London, 1855. Cited as Keightley, *Life*.

Masson, D. *Life and Times of John Milton*, rev. ed., 6 vols., London, 1881. Cited as Masson, *Life*.

Peck, F. *New Memoirs of the Life and Poetical Works of Mr. John Milton*, London, 1740.

Philips, E. *Life of Milton*. See Godwin, *Lives of Edward and John Philips, Appendix II*.

Richardson, J. *Explanatory Notes and Remarks on Milton's Paradise Lost, by J. Richardson, Father and Son, with a Life of the Author and a Discourse on the Poem by F. Richardson, Sen.* London, 1734. Cited as *Richardson*.

Stern, A. *Milton und seine Zeit*, 2 vols., Leipzig, 1877-1879.

Todd, H. J. *Some Account of the Life and Writings of John Milton*, London, 1826. Cited as Todd, *Life*.

Toland, J. *Life of John Milton*, London, 1699 ; repr. 1761. Cited as Toland, *Life*.

2. Editions of Milton's Works

Browne, R. C. *English Poems*, 2 vols., Oxford, 1875-1878.

Browning, O. *Tractate on Education*, Cambridge, 1905.

Collins, J. C. *Samson Agonistes*, Oxford, 1906.

Cowper, W. *Milton's Latin and Italian Poems Translated into English Verse*, ed. W. Hayley, Chichester, 1810. Cited as *Cowper*.

Facsimile of the MS. of Milton's Minor Poems, Preserved in the Library of Trinity College, Cambridge, Cambridge, 1899. Cited as *Cambridge Facsimile.*

HORWOOD, A. J. *Commonplace Book, and a Latin Essay and Latin Verses presumed to be by Milton,* Westminster, 1876. Cited as *Commonplace Book.*

JERRAM, C. S. *Paradise Regained,* New York, 1902.

— *Samson Agonistes,* London, 1890.

MASSON, D. *Poetical Works,* 3 vols., London, 1893.

PATTISON, M. *Sonnets,* London, 1883. Cited as *Pattison.*

ST. JOHN, J. A. *Prose Works,* 5 vols., London, 1853. Cited as *P.W.*

SYMMONS, C. *Prose Works,* 7 vols. London, 1806.

TODD, H. J. *Poetical Works,* 7 vols., London, 1809.

VERITY, A. W. *Arcades,* Cambridge, 1906.

— *Ode on the Morning of Christ's Nativity, L'Allegro, Il Penseroso, and Lycidas,* Cambridge, 1906.

— *Arcades and Comus,* Cambridge, 1891.

— *Sonnets,* Cambridge, 1895.

— *Paradise Lost,* 6 vols., Cambridge, 1892-1905.

— *Samson Agonistes,* Cambridge, 1897.

WARTON, T. *Poems, English, Italian, and Latin, with Translations,* London, 1791.

3. SPECIAL STUDIES, ETC.

BRADSHAW, J. *A Concordance to the Poetical Works of John Milton,* New York, 1894.

COOK, A. S. *Notes on Milton's Ode on the Morning of Christ's Nativity,* repr. from *Transactions of the Connecticut Academy,* 15. 308-368, 1909.

LOCKWOOD, L. E. *Lexicon to the English Poetical Works of John Milton,* New York, London, 1907.

ORCHARD, T. N. *The Astronomy of Milton's Paradise Lost,* London, New York, Bombay, 1896.

OSGOOD, C. G. *The Classical Mythology of Milton's English Poems,* New York, 1900. Cited as Osgood, *Mythology.*

SCHLESINGER, F. A. *Der Natursinn bei John Milton,* Leipzig, 1892.

4. SOURCES OF MILTON'S THEORIES

AMBROSIUS, *Enarrationes in XII Psalmos Davidicos.* See Migne, *Patrologia Latina.*

ARISTOTLE, *Opera, ed. Academia Regia Borussica,* 5 vols., Berlin, 1831-1870. Cited as *Aristotle.*

ARISTOTLE, *Politics*. translated by B. Jowett, Oxford, 1905.

ARISTOXENUS, *Harmonics*, ed. with Translation, Notes, Introduction and Index of Words by H. S. Macran, Oxford, 1902. Cited as *Aristoxenus*.

BOETHIUS, A. M. S. *Über die Musik*, ed. Oscar Paul, Leipzig, 1872. Cited as Boethius, *De Musica*.

CICERO, *Somnium Scipionis*, tr. by C. R. Edmonds, *Cicero's Three Books of Offices*, pp. 288-305, Bohn Library, London, 1887.

JAN, K. *Musici Scriptores Graeci*, Leipzig, 1899.

KIRCHER, A. *Musurgia Universalis, sive Ars Magna Consoni et Dissoni*, 2 vols., Rome, 1650. Cited as Kircher, *Mus. Univ.*

MACROBIUS, A. A. T. *Opera*, ed. F. Eyssenhardt, Leipzig, 1893. Cited as *Macrobius*.

MARTIANUS CAPELLA. *De Nuptiis Philologiae et Mercurii*, ed. F. Eyssenhardt, Leipzig, 1866.

MEIBOM, M. *Antiquae Musicae Auctores Septem*, 2 vols., Amsterdam, 1652.

MIGNE, J. P. *Patrologia Latina*, 161 vols. Paris, 1857-80.

MORLEY, T. *A Plain and Easy Introduction to Practical Music* (1597), repr. London, 1771. Cited as *Morley*.

PHILO JUDAEUS, *Works*, Translated from the Greek by C. D. Yonge, 4 vols., London, 1854-1855.

PLATO, *Dialogues*, Translated into English by B. Jowett, Oxford, 1875.

PLINIUS SECUNDUS, C. *Natural History*, Translated by J. Bostock and H. T. Riley, 6 vols., London, 1856-1893.

PLUTARCH, *De Musica*, ed. R. Westphal, (text, translation, and notes,) Leipzig, n. d. Cited as *Plutarch*.

PROCLUS, *On the Theology of Plato*, ed. J. Creuzer, 3 vols., Frankfurt, 1820-22.

TINCTORIS, J. *Tractatus de Musica*, ed. E. de Coussemaker, Lille, 1875.

5. HISTORICAL WORKS ON MUSIC

ABERT, H. *Die Musikanschauung des Mittelalters*, Halle, 1905.

BURNEY, C. *A General History of Music from the Earliest Ages to the Present Period*, 4 vols., London, 1776-1789. Cited as *Burney*.

CHAPPELL, W. *Old English Popular Music*, ed. H. E. Wooldridge 2 vols., London, 1893. Cited as *Chappell*.

DAVEY, H. *History of English Music*, London, 1895. Cited as *Davey*.

GEVAERT, F. A. *La Musique de l'Antiquité,* 2 vols., Gand, 1875.

GLEDITSCH, H. *Die Musik der Griechen, Anhang* in *Handbuch d. Klassischen Altertumswissenschaft* 2. 3. München, 1901.

HAWKINS, J. *A General History of the Science and Practice of Music,* 5 vols., London, 1776. Cited as *Hawkins.*

HOPE, R. C. *Mediœval Music,* London, 1894.

MONRO, D. B. *The Modes of Ancient Greek Music,* Oxford, 1894.

Oxford History of Music, vols. 1 and 3, Oxford, 1901-1902.

RITTER, A. G. *Zur Geschichte des Orgelspiels,* Leipzig, 1884.

WESTPHAL, R. *Die Musik des Griechischen Alterthumes,* Leipzig, 1883.

WILLIAMS, C. F. A. *The Story of the Organ,* London, 1903.

6. MISCELLANEOUS

ADEMOLLO, A. *La Leonora di Milton e di Clemente IX.,* Milano, n. d.

BECKER, C. F. *Systematische Chronologische Darstellung d. Musikalischen Literatur,* Leipzig, 1836.

BECKER, C. F. *Die Tonwerke d. XVI. u. XVII. Jahrhunderts,* Leipzig, 1855.

BURNET, J. *Early Greek Philosophy,* London, 1908.

DICKINSON, G. L. *The Greek View of Life,* London, 1905.

GROVE, G. *Dictionary of Music and Musicians,* ed. J. A. F. Maitland, 5 vols., New York. 1904-1909. Cited as Grove's *Dict.*

HUTCHINSON, Lucy. *Memoirs of the Life of Colonel Hutchinson,* London, 1848.

MATHEW, J. E. *A Handbook of Musical History and Bibliography,* London, 1898.

PATER, W. *Plato and Platonism,* New York, 1903.

PEACHAM, H. *The Compleat Gentleman,* ed. G. S. Gordon, Oxford, 1906. Cited as *Compleat Gentleman.*

PRYNNE, W. *Histriomastix, The Players' Scourge or Actors' Tragaedie,* London, 1633. Cited as *Histriomastix.*

INDEX